The Sword Verse:

Qur'ānic Weapon Against Peace?

Other Books in this Series

***The Qur'ān**: Its View and Treatment of Non-Muslims*

A study of its ninth chapter, or sūra al-Tawba (the basis for Islam's perception, value judgments, and dealings with all other religions and their followers), traces how Islam's view and treatment of non-Muslims negatively changed over time.

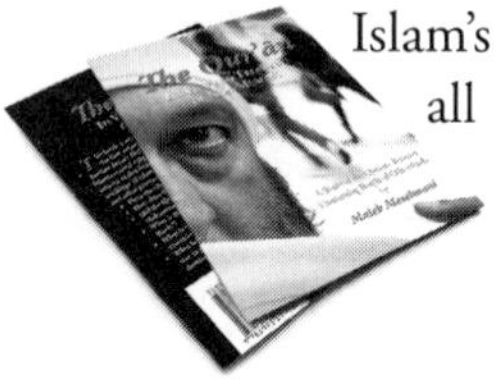

(32 pp., $6.95) ISBN: 978-1-935577-08-9

Women in Islam: Honored or Persecuted?

The Qur'ān, the source of all personal status laws in Islamic countries, gives men supreme authority over women, with rulings prescribing fewer privileges and options for women in such matters as marital and legal rights, inheritance, and the afterlife.

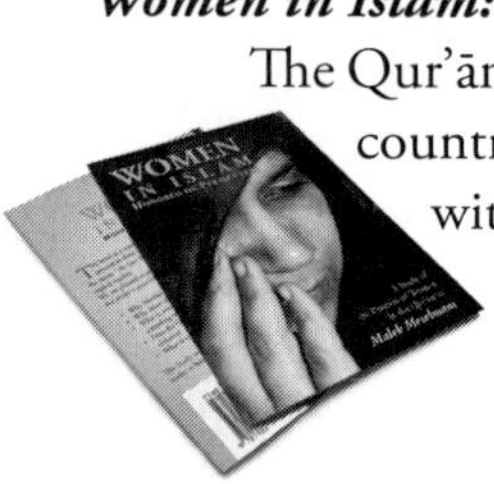

(32 pp., $6.95) ISBN: 978-1-935577-07-2

***Taqīya**: Deliberate Deception*

The principle of *taqīya* and its application is inherent in the Islam world. Characterized as "double-speak" by one critic and lauded by Shiite scholars as the "believer's paradise," the practice of *taqīya* since the time of Muhammad has profoundly impacted Islamic politics, culture, and society.

(84 pp., $9.95) ISBN: 978-1-935577-09-6

The Sword Verse:

Qur'ānic Weapon Against Peace?

by

Malek Meselmani

Printed in USA.

WLP Reference: 201504-04-10000
ISBN: 978-1-935577-33-1

For permission requests, e-mail ***permissions@waterlifepublishing.com*** with the following subject line:

Attention: "The Sword Verse: Quranic Weapon" Permissions Coordinator.

ORDERING INFORMATION

Special discounts are available on quantity purchases by corporations, associations, and other organizations.

For details, contact ***orders@waterlifepublishing.com*** with the following subject line: Attention: "The Sword Verse: Quranic Weapon" Quantity Purchases.

U.S. trade bookstores and wholesalers should contact ***orders@waterlifepublishing.com*** with the following subject line:
Attention: "The Sword Verse: Quranic Weapon" Distribution.

For more information, please visit
www.waterlifepublishing.com

OR telephone
+1-206-973-3235 USA

Contents

Resources and References

The Sword Verse:
Qur'ānic Weapon Against Peace?

One of the most famous verses in the Qur'ān is called the Sword verse. It is the verse that commands Muslims to kill non-Muslims: "*...slay the idolaters wherever you find them, and take them, and confine them, and lie in wait for them at every place of ambush...*" (Arberry trans. Q 9.5).

The thoughtful reader of the Qur'ān will probably pause in confusion, for how does one reconcile this verse with tens of other verses that call for tolerance, such as Q 2.256 (Pickthall trans.): "There is no compulsion in religion...." The baffled reader encounters two contrasting spirits, as if facing the conflicted protagonist of Robert Louis Stevenson's novella *The Strange Case of Dr. Jekyll and Mr. Hyde*. A kind of schizophrenia seems incarnated in the Qur'ān with its verses of peace (which resemble the character of Dr. Jekyll) and its verses of killing (which reflect the character of Mr. Hyde), and the reader is left to ponder these questions:

- Why does the Qur'ān's text present a double personality?
- How can a Muslim take the Qur'ān as the guide for living one's life when it has two contrasting spirits?
- Which should the Muslim follow: the verses that reflect Jekyll or Hyde?

Muslim scholars do not see the Qur'ān as a book with two opposing positions. Rather, they state that the Qur'ān consists of abrogating and abrogated verses.* (Abrogated verses are verses that have been nullified or overridden by other verses, the abrogating verses. See "Special Names and Terms, page 107.) According to Qur'ānic scholar al-Zarkashī, most Islamic sources state that the Sword verse itself has abrogated, or nullified, 114 verses that call for making peace with non-Muslims and to leave them alone in peace.[1] (See the table "Qur'ānic Verses Abrogated by the Sword Verse," page 55.) According to the Islamic commentators, whenever there are two contrasting texts, such as Q 2.256 (Arberry trans.: *"No compulsion is there in religion..."*) and Q 9.5 (*"...slay the idolaters wherever you find them..."*), the Muslim should follow the ruling in the verse that was revealed later to Muḥammad, the founder and prophet of Islam. In this case, Q 9.5 abrogates Q 2.256, because Q 9.5 came later, during the Medinan period.* Since virtually all the pacifist texts were revealed during the earlier Meccan period,* they have been abrogated by the later warlike Medinan texts. In this way, the process of abrogation thus resolves the conflict between these two types of verses and forces the tenor and attitude of the Qur'ān's verses to change over time—and with it, Muḥammad's actions—from tolerance to fanaticism, from tongue to sword, from peace to war.

Historical Overview

According to Islamic tradition, Muḥammad received his first Qur'ānic revelation in AD 610 and continued to receive more revelations for the next twenty-three years until shortly before his death. Throughout these years, Muḥammad experienced many political and social changes, which are echoed in the Qur'ān and reflect the circumstances of his call in Mecca and Medina.

To best understand the revelation and role of the Sword verse, one must examine the two major periods—Meccan and Medinan—of Muḥammad's call. The Qur'ānic revelations of these two periods are markedly different, with the later Medinan verses and Muḥammad's followers increasingly more violent in tone, attitude, and action.

Meccan Period (c. 12 BH-AH 1/AD 610-622)

After several years of his Da'wa,* or call, Muḥammad realized that his hope of winning the Quraysh tribe to his new religion was unlikely, because he had only gathered together a meager number of believers. His dejection over this situation was compounded by his shock and despair over the death of his wife Khadīja, followed only a few weeks later by his uncle Abū Ṭālib Ibn 'Abd al-Muṭṭalib (3 BH/AD 619). Both of them were extremely important to Muḥammad. Not only was Khadīja his psychological and financial supporter, she was his first convert and an encouraging helper. Abū Ṭālib, the leader of the Banū Hāshim (a clan of the Quraysh), was Muḥammad's shield in the face of any Quraysh threat. Through Muḥammad's familial ties with his paternal uncle Abū Ṭālib, Muḥammad (an orphan) received tribal protection, in accordance to tribal tradition: no one could harass him with impunity. Thus, the deaths of these key people in his life—his wife and his "surrogate father"—must undoubtedly have destabilized Muḥammad's psychological (if not physical) well-being, leaving him feeling vulnerable and alone.[2]

Without Khadīja's support and Abū Ṭālib's protection, Muḥammad became even more desperate to win over the Quraysh. He began preaching among Mecca's visitors, offering his religion to various Arab tribes.[3] After three more years of desperate struggle to spread his call in Mecca, Muḥammad met the people of Medina (known as the Yathrib before Islam). After a series of meetings between the two parties, the Medinan people agreed to receive the Muslims into their city. It is at this point, according to Islamic sources, that the first verse to state a declaration of war against the enemies of Islam was "revealed" to Muḥammad: *"Leave is given to those who fight because they were wronged—surely God is able to help them—"* (Q 22.39).[4] The timing and tone of this verse indicate that the change of Muḥammad's political circumstances provided him with the opportunity to switch his strategies to advance his religion.

When Muḥammad and his followers eventually migrated to Medina, he was mentally defeated by his great failure to win over the Quraysh to Islam. He left Mecca amid accusations by the Quraysh tribesmen that he was "bewitched" (see Yusuf Ali trans. Q 17.47, Q 25.8), a *"lying sorcerer"* (see Arberry trans. Q 38.4) and a man *"possessed"* (see Q 68.51, Q 15.6). In Q 81.22 (*"Your companion is not possessed"*) acknowledges these same accusations by claiming in this verse that Muḥammad is sane. Such public cynicism must have caused him nightmares and sleepless nights. The Quraysh's opinion that Muḥammad was too inferior to be a messenger from heaven is apparent in their disdainful, sarcastic comments, such as "Among all the creation of God, is this the messenger that he has sent?"[5] and referenced in Q 25.41: *"And when they see thee, they take thee in mockery only: 'What, is this he whom God sent forth as a Messenger?'"* where the Arabic expression *'āhazā* ("is this one") in this context connotes contempt for Muḥammad.[6]

Medinan Period (AH 1-11/AD 622-632)

When Muḥammad and his small band of followers migrated to Medina, they experienced difficulties in finding work similar to what they had done in Mecca, a trading-based economy. Lacking the necessary skills and resources to participate or complement the economy of Medina, these Emigrants* (Muslims from Mecca) could not adequately contribute to their own subsistence, creating a burden on the city. In addition to this problem, some of the Medinan people did not welcome the Emigrants, even though they pretended that they had accepted Islam. For this reason, these Medinan skeptics were labeled and decried as hypocrites* (*al-munāfiqūn*) by the Emigrants.

As time passed and the Emigrants' failed to integrate themselves within the Medinan economy, they decided to form raiding parties to rob passing caravans, because of their economic destitution and their hatred for the people of Mecca. The Emigrants blamed the Meccans for their move from Mecca and their humiliating economic circumstances in this foreign city of Medina. The Qur'ān (Q 9.14-15) reveals the degree of this hatred in the hearts of the Emigrants:

> *Fight them, and God will chastise them at your hands and degrade them, and He will help you against them, and bring healing to the breasts of a people who believe, / and He will remove the rage within their hearts; and God turns towards whomsoever He will; God is All-knowing, All-wise.*

These verses state that God's punishment will be administered by the hands of the Muslims themselves on their enemies, and, in the process, God will remove all hatred and distress from the faithful people (Muslims).

This transformation of the Emigrants from law-abiding merchants into predatory raiders marks a major turning point in the history of the Arabian Peninsula. For these early Muslims, this transformation created the beginning nucleus of a military force, which would eventually grow in size and power to enable Muḥammad to unify all of Arabia into one religious polity (AH 11/AD 632). However, the means for this military development by the

Emigrants—the raiding, looting, and killing—introduced a decline in the moral values (e.g., religious tolerance) the Muslims had advocated and held up to the pagan Arabs to denounce their polytheistic and sinful religious and social practices.

This moral decline began with the commencement of raiding parties, which were initiated after the Emigrants were living in Medina. During one scouting expedition, 'Abd Allah Ibn Jaḥsh, Muḥammad's cousin, attacked a Quraysh commercial caravan during a month sacred to the Arabs, a time when battles and bloodshed were prohibited. This raid, which resulted in fighting and a man's death, raised concerns among the Muslims. To ease their anxiety, Muḥammad "revealed" Q 2.217, which supports[7] his cousin's action:

> *They will question thee concerning the holy month, and fighting in it. Say: 'Fighting in it is a heinous thing, but to bar from God's way, and disbelief in Him, and the Holy Mosque, and to expel its people from it—that is more heinous in God's sight; and persecution is more heinous than slaying'....*

With this Qur'ānic text, Muḥammad absolved 'Abd Allah Ibn Jaḥsh and justified his raiders' killing and looting during a sacred month because the victims were unbelievers, i.e., non-Muslims who might seduce or drive Muslims away from Allah. This "excused" breach of committing bloodshed during a sacred month became the starting point for more violence and raids, and, later, invasions by these early Muslims.

Barbarity

Soon after this raid, the Muslims fought their first pitched battle (AH 2/AD 624) against the Quraysh tribesmen in Badr and achieved their first victory against them. One narration of this battle discusses in detail the killing of one of Muḥammad's archenemies, the Quraysh leader, 'Amr Ibn Hishām[8] or "Abū al-Ḥakam" ("Father of Wisdom"), so named by his tribe because of his keen intelligence and leadership skills. (Islamic sources refer to this man, a contemporary and relentless, fierce critic of Muḥammad, as "Abū Jaḥl," which means "Father of Ignorance.")

During the Battle of Badr two Muslim warriors separately attacked Abū al-Ḥakam. One of them sliced off Abū al-Ḥakam's lower leg with his sword. The other stabbed Abū al-Ḥakam while he lay on the ground. Mortally wounded, Abū al-Ḥakam was approached by 'Abd Allah Ibn Mas'ūd, one of Muḥammad's closest Companions,* after the end of the battle. As Abū al-Ḥakam was taking his final breaths, Ibn Mas'ūd placed his foot on the neck of the dying man and stated, "Has God [Allah] put you to shame, you enemy of God?" to which Abū al-Ḥakam defiantly replied, "How has He [Allah] shamed me? Am I anything more remarkable than a man you have killed? Tell me how the battle went." When Ibn Mas'ūd told Abū al-Ḥakam that Allah and his messenger (Muḥammad) had won the battle, Abū al-Ḥakam spoke his last words: "You have climbed high, you little shepherd." (As a youth, Ibn Mas'ūd had tended the flocks of a Quraysh chieftain.) Abū al-Ḥakam's final words both mocked and rebuked Ibn Mas'ūd for asserting his superiority when he was about to kill a defenseless, dying man. Ibn Masʿūd stated that he then cut off Abū al-Ḥakam's head and threw it into the hands of Muḥammad, who gave thanks and praise to Allah.[9]

By expressing nothing but support, joy, and thanksgiving for the beheading of a wounded man, Muḥammad set an example not only for the early Muslim followers but for jihadists of today who never hesitate to kill the wounded. (Indeed, these jihadists rush to commit the heinous act of beheading people as part of their strategy to intimidate and subdue their enemies.) Furthermore, this moral descent into barbarity also established a trend among these early Muslims to mutilate their enemies in a manner and an intensity that far exceeded the warfare practices of tribal chieftains of that time.

Another example of this growing barbarity, recounted repeatedly in the Islamic sources, concerns an old woman named Faṭima Bint Rabīʿa, or, more simply, Umm Qirfa.[10] She held an honored position among her people, the Banū Fazāra, in Wādī al-Qurā, near Medina. This tribe vehemently resisted Islam. In a skirmish with Zayd Ibn Ḥāritha, Muḥammad's adopted son, in AH 6 (AD 627), the tribe succeeded in killing some Muslims and wounding Zayd. Zayd swore revenge and returned several months later to Wādī al-Qurā with a larger force. He defeated the tribe, killing most of the men and capturing many of the women and children, including Umm Qirfa. Though very old, Umm Qirfa was put to death in a most cruel, horrific way by the victorious Muslim force. According to several Islamic accounts, Umm Qirfa was torn apart after being tied between two strong young camels.[11] This brutal execution was ordered by Zayd Ibn Ḥāritha.[12]

Not even one condemnation was heard from Muḥammad or from any of his elder Companions (Abū Bakr, ʻUmar Ibn al-Khaṭṭāb, or ʻAlī Ibn Abī Ṭālib) for this heinous act. Indeed, when Zayd returned to tell Muḥammad about the success of his raid, Muḥammad hurriedly dragged on "his clothes which he had put off" upon hearing Zayd's knock, so eager was he to embrace and kiss Zayd.[13]

Zaynab's Return to Medina: Two Responses

The despicably savage killing of Umm Qirfa by the Muslims contrasts sharply with the incredibly humane treatment of Zaynab, Muḥammad's eldest daughter, by the Quraysh (Muḥammad's foremost enemy) as related in another narrative included in the Islamic sources.[14] In this recount, Zaynab tried to free her polytheistic husband Abū al-ʻĀs, who was captured during the Battle of Badr by her father's forces. She sent her father Muḥammad ransom money and the wedding gift—a necklace—given to her by her mother Khadīja. Muḥammad allowed Abū al-ʻĀs to return to Mecca but requested that Zaynab come to him in Medina. While preparing for this trip, Zaynab was approached by the wife of Meccan leader Abū Sufyān, Hind Bint ʻUtba, who offered her assistance, but Zaynab rebuffed her, fearing her intentions.

Zaynab departed Mecca in broad daylight, accompanied by her brother-in-law, Kināna Ibn al-Rabīʻ, to protect her from possible harm by the Quraysh. The Quraysh, learning of their departure, rushed after them in pursuit.

When the first Quraysh man to reach them threatened her safety with his lance, Kināna challenged him. Then Abū Sufyān and other Quraysh leaders rode up and told Kināna that they intended Zaynab no harm or to keep her from her father. However, they told Kināna that he and Zaynab should not have been so public about their travel, which would be viewed as an insensitive affront to the Quraysh people, reminding them of their "humiliation after the disaster that has happened [Battle of Badr] and an exhibition of utter weakness."[15] Abū Sufyān counseled Kināna to return Zaynab back to Mecca and then leave at a later date, in secret, so that the Quraysh could save face. Kināna followed this advice and took Zaynab back to Mecca. He later delivered Zaynab safely during the night to Zayd Ibn Ḥāritha, who then took her to her father Muḥammad.

The only possible harm that befell Zaynab during this incident is an allegation ("It is alleged…") that she was pregnant and miscarried when the first Quraysh riders frightened her.[16] The Islamic sources, however, do record Hind Bint 'Utba's response to the returning Quraysh riders, and it is critical of their initial intimidation of Zaynab: "In peace are you wild asses—rough and coarse / And in war like women in their courses [menstruating women]?"[17]

Her insulting comments and disapproval of her own tribesmen's behavior toward Zaynab are noteworthy and illuminating. Instead of supporting her Quraysh tribesmen, Hind Bint 'Utba rebuked them for their threatening behavior toward Zaynab, who was not just any woman but a daughter of Muḥammad, who just defeated them at the Battle of Badr and was their mortal enemy. Her condemnation of a verbal threat (as none of the riders even touched Zaynab) and the Quraysh riders' generally benign treatment of Zaynab provide a powerful example of the Quraysh's moral code of behavior—even when at war.

Compare Muḥammad's response to this incident. Instead of expressing gratitude or relief upon his daughter's safe arrival to Medina, Muḥammad ordered raiders to accost the first Quraysh riders who verbally threatened Zaynab and "burn them with fire."[18] After a day's reflection, Muḥammad revised his order. He told his raiders "that none has the right to punish by fire save God [Allah], so if you capture them kill them."[19] In either case, Muḥammad's punitive action seems extremely vindictive and unjust, given the circumstances and outcome of this particular incident.

Sexual Violence

Unfortunately, the cowardly killing of Abū al-Ḥakam and the atrocity of Umm Qirfa's death were not exceptional cases. Many other narrations describe similar acts committed by the early Muslims against their perceived enemies. The danger of these acts is not that they signal a declination of the moral values that existed before Islam. The real danger is that the sacred texts of the Muslims (Qur'ān and Ḥadīth literature*) were used to justify these violations to infuse the confidence, remove the anxiety, and relieve the conscience of the faithful.

Not only did this justification make the encouragement of violence and fighting against non-Muslims a religiously lawful act, it also permitted Muslims to violate the bodies of female captives.

Instances of this kind of sexual abuse have been recorded by Islamic scholars. In one account, the Muslims took six thousand hostages[20] on the day of the Battle of Ḥunayn (AH 8/AD 630), including "married women from the women of the People of the Book."[21] (In the Qur'ān, the term "People of the Book" refers to Jews and Christians.) However, the Muslim warriors were loath to have sexual intercourse with their married female captives.[22] When they consulted Muḥammad regarding this matter, he responded with Q 4.24 (Hilâlî-Khân trans.): "Also (forbidden are) women already married, except those (captives and slaves) whom your right hands possess...." After hearing this verse, one of the Muslims stated, "We have made their vulvae lawful to us."[23] Thus, this Qur'ānic verse makes it lawful—in the name of Allah himself—to sexually "enjoy," i.e., rape, these enslaved women, regardless of their marital status.

Based on the hostage situation following the Battle of Ḥunayn and the subsequent revelation of Q 4.24, Islam initiated rulings whereby the captive woman is sexually available to her owner, though scholars differ as to when the first intercourse after her captivity is permitted—before or after she menstruates.[24] Furthermore, these rulings allow the Muslim man to sexually "enjoy" his female slave even if she is married. One Shiite religious opinion states that if a Muslim man owns a married slave couple, the owner has the right to sexually enjoy the female by requesting her slave husband to isolate his wife until she menstruates. Then the owner can have sexual intercourse with her. Once she menstruates after he is finished with her, "he sends her back without another intercourse with her."[25]

These specific rulings regarding the sexual treatment of captive women diverged from the moral code of behavior of the early Muslims, who followed the moral conscience of their pagan communities up to that time. Muḥammad, through these changes and their acceptance by his followers, produced a doctrine that succeeded in disrupting (if not corrupting) this moral conscience.

Infidels and the Final Solution

In Medina, Muḥammad declared that it is a Muslim's duty to fight the polytheists: *"Fight them* [*"the unbelievers"*; see Q 8.38] *till there is no persecution and the religion is God's entirely; then if they give over, surely God sees the things they do"* (Arberry trans. Q 8.39). This verse's meaning coincides with the words of Muḥammad in a *ḥadīth**: "I have been commanded to fight against people till they testify that there is no god but Allah."[26] Both Q 8.39 and this *ḥadīth* indicate that the reason for the fighting is the polytheists' unbelief in Islam. Similarly, Q 8.39 matches in meaning with Q 2.193: *"Fight them, till there is no persecution and the religion is God's; then if they give over, there shall be no enmity save for evildoers."* Therefore, in accordance to the rule that is established in this verse, the infidels' unbelief can only end with the acceptance of Islam—or death by killing.

This directive in Q 8.39 to fight non-Muslims until they accept Islam is bolstered by the Sword verse and other fighting verses in sura Tawba (Q 9), considered by most Islamic accounts as the last revealed chapter in the Qur'ān. As the supposedly final verses of the Qur'ān, these verses then carry the ultimate power because they are, in essence, the final (abrogating) word.

Challenges to the Sword Verse

The commands for violence in the Sword verse target *"idolaters,"* or nonbelievers of Islam. In recent times, some Muslim scholars and leaders will claim that the focus of these violent commands is countered by opposing verses from the Qur'ān, such as Q 2.256 (Pickthall trans.):[27]

> **There is no compulsion in religion**. The right direction is henceforth distinct from error. And he who rejecteth false deities and believeth in Allah hath grasped a firm handhold which will never break. Allah is Hearer, Knower. (emphasis added)

No Compulsion in Religion

Can Q 2.256 be considered a verse that allows freedom of religion and establishes the principle that Islam cannot force its religion on others, especially since this verse is included in a Medinan sura (and thus protected from abrogation)?

The answer to this question can be derived from studying the historical background and context of this verse, or what is known in the Qur'ānic literature as *asbāb al-nuzūl*, the occasions* or circumstances of revelation.

These occasions describe the causes or details of the incidents that immediately preceded the revelation of a given verse.

By studying the occasion of this particular verse Q 2.256, two main possible stories (with some variations) emerge from the literature.

Muslim Father with Two Christian Sons (Occasion A)
In this occasion, a Muslim man (one of *al-Anṣār** or "the Helpers") called al-Ḥuṣayn had two Christian sons who refused to convert to Islam. He asked Muḥammad if he should coerce his sons to accept Islam. In response, Muḥammad recited to him Q 2.256.[28] A similar narration states that the man's two sons became Christians at the hands of some traders from the Levant (eastern Mediterranean region) and later joined the traders. The father came to Muḥammad to complain and to have Muḥammad send someone to bring his sons back. Instead, Muḥammad recites to the father Q 2.256.[29]

Medinan Jewish Children (Occasions B1 and B2)
Islamic narrations explain that if a pagan woman of Medina bore children who never survived, she might promise God that if she bore a child who did survive, she would allow Jews to adopt and raise her child, because the Medinan people (before their conversion to Islam) believed that Judaism was better than paganism.

According to this occasion of Q 2.256, Muḥammad surrounded the Jewish fortresses of Banū al-Naḍīr, located on the oasis of Medina, during his conflicts with tribes who rejected his religion. (The year was AH 4, or AD 626, after Islam's advent into Medina.) When the Jews of Banū al-Naḍīr surrendered to Muḥammad, he commanded them to evacuate their fortresses, expatriating them from their lands. Among the Banū al-Naḍīr were Medinan Jewish adoptees, whose adoptive Jewish families wanted to keep them. However, the Medinan birth families objected to this plan; they did not want the adoptees to be deported with their Jewish families and told Muḥammad, "Don't let our children go!" Muḥammad's response was Q 2.256.[30] To this verse, Muḥammad added, "Make your children decide: if they choose you, they become one of you, and if they choose the others [Jews], **have them evacuated with them**" (emphasis added).[31] In other words, Muḥammad told the 'Anṣār, "Who[ever] wishes can follow them [Jews], and who[ever] wishes [to stay with their birth families] enters Islam."[32] So, based on this occasion, the "freedom" allowed to these Medinan Jewish adoptees is deportation with the Banū al-Naḍīr or conversion to Islam.

A variation of this occasion is recorded by Islamic commentator al-Ṭabarī, who states that the Medinan people who had their children adopted and raised by Jews asked Muḥammad (after his arrival to their city), if they had to coerce their now Jewish-adopted children to convert to Islam. (These Medinan people were now 'Anṣār.) To this inquiry, Muḥammad responded with Q 2.256. Al-Ṭabarī does not place the time of revelation for this verse with the incident of the Banū al-Naḍīr evacuation; rather, it comes in the context of an answer to the question of whether the 'Anṣār should compel their children to leave Judaism. In that context, the verse must have come before AH 4 (AD 626), the year of the deportation of the Banū al-Naḍīr Jews, and perhaps even before the Hijra* (the migration of Muḥammad and his followers from Mecca to Medina in AH 1). Al-Ṭabarī's commentary indicates convincingly that this verse Q 2.256 is Meccan:[33]

> The Messenger of Allah…was in Mecca for ten years, and he did not coerce anyone to come to his religion. Yet the polytheists still wanted to fight them, so he asked permission from Allah to fight them back, and Allah authorized him.

Regardless of the time of its revelation, this occasion—implied here as Meccan—considers that the "no-compulsion" principle was only applied during the Meccan era and should not be treated as a general rule.

Q 2.256
No Compulsion in Religion

Occasion A

Muslim father of two Christian sons, who asks Muḥammad for his help to convert/return them.

Occasion B1

Medinan Anṣār birth parents ask Muḥammad to let their Jewish-adopted children—now Jewish adoptees—remain and not leave with the exiled Jews of Banū al-Naḍīr. (AH 4/AD 625)

Occasion B2

Medinan people who had given up their children for Jewish adoption ask Muḥammad if they should force these children to convert to Islam, now that they, the birth parents, have become Muslims. (c. AH 2/AD 624)

Analysis of the Occasions of Q 2.256

Even though these narrations (and their variations) concern a specific event, it is possible that Muḥammad responded to the Muslim father (Occasion A) with a Meccan-revealed verse but then repeated this same Meccan verse when he was in Medina responding to the birth parents of their Jewish-adopted children (Occasion B). Also, one could hypothesize that al-Ḥuṣayn came to Muḥammad, expecting divine help with the prophet's intercession. When Muḥammad could not provide this divine assistance, he gave al-Ḥuṣayn this verse instead.

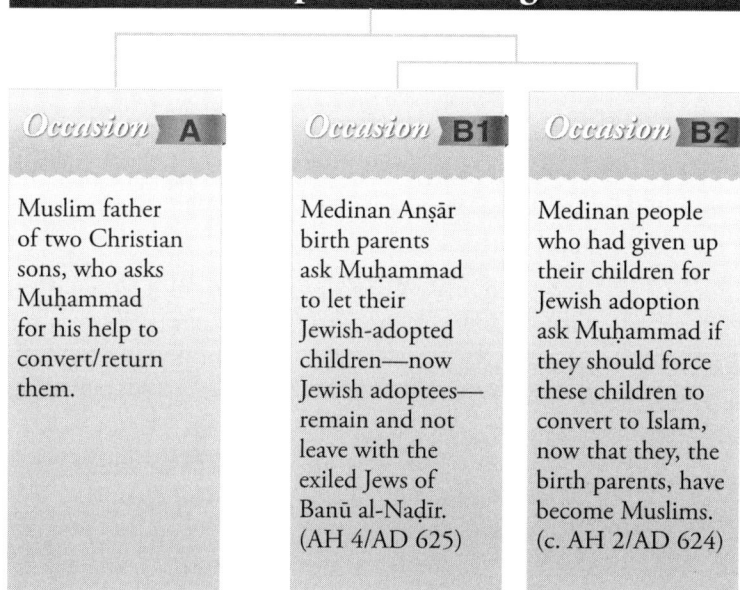

However, sura Baqara (Q 2) is considered a Medinan chapter, so one must accept the possibility that Q 2.256 may be a Medinan verse and review its two major possible occasions from that perspective.

Regretfully, Occasion A, which concerns the Muslim father and his two Christian sons, has no specific details to help place the time of revelation for Q 2.256. Even if Q 2.256 is truly a Medinan-revealed verse, the "no-compulsion" principle in the verse has been abrogated with the subsequent fighting verses, according to Islamic scholar al-Wāḥidī. After narrating the occasion describing how the sons of al-Ḥuṣayn converted to Christianity, he states this caveat:[34]

> **This** [rule in Q 2.256] **was before the Messenger of Allah was commanded…to fight the People of the Book. But then the verse** ("No compulsion in religion") **was abrogated and the Prophet was commanded to fight the People of the Book in sura al-Tawba** [Q 9]**.** (emphasis added)

Unlike the narration concerning the Muslim father and his two Christian sons, Occasion B2 (newly Muslim Medinan birth parents ask if they must coerce their children—now Jewish adoptees—to convert to Islam) does include some details to suggest an approximate time frame for its narration. Based on these details, it is very likely that Muḥammad's answer to the 'Anṣār came soon after his entrance into Medina, when Muḥammad initially sought to gain the allegiance—if not acceptance—of the Medinan Jews during the first two years of his Da'wa there. The first public signs of his disenchantment with the Medinan Jews because of their dismissal of him came less than two years after the Hijra (AH 2/AD 624), when Muḥammad suddenly changed the *qiblah* (direction to face when praying) to Mecca instead of Jerusalem, the holiest city for Jews.[35]

Given this two-year time frame and even more details included in Occasion B1 (Medinan 'Anṣār birth parents ask that their adopted children be excluded from the Banū al-Naḍīr evacuation), the earliest possible date for Q 2.256 would be the recorded evacuation of Banū al-Naḍīr, or August AH 4 (AD 625).[36] At that time, Muḥammad had not yet consolidated his power in Medina, as Medina was still not exclusive to Muḥammad and the Muslims. He was opposed by a strong group, called "the hypocrites" in the Islamic sources, and his movement had no formidable striking army—yet. In fact, a Muslim force had experienced a serious setback a few months earlier during the Battle of Uḥud (March of AH 3/AD 625). Muḥammad was seriously wounded, and his death then undoubtedly would have resulted in the collapse of the Islamic movement.

As Muḥammad recovered from his wounds, he gained power, and, with it, displayed increasingly greater belligerence toward his perceived enemies. Once he attained sufficient control of Medina, Muḥammad expelled the Jewish presence from the city through deportation and extermination, justifying this policy with "combat" texts, such as the Sword verse (Q 9.5) and a fighting verse Q 9.29, both of which have abrogated dozens of pacifist and other tolerance-leaning verses, including Q 2.256.

The difference between Occasions B1 and B2 is that Muhammad pressed for conversion of the Jewish adoptees in B1. However, he did not force coercion at that time because he had not yet legalized the Sword verse or the fighting verses. **Yet, in both versions of this occasion, Muḥammad's stance was not free of coercion, as he declared that the children must chose between their adoptive Jewish families (and evacuation from Medina) or their birth families (and conversion to Islam).**[37]

Do these choices truly represent no compulsion in religion?

It may be moot to determine if Q 2.256 is a Meccan or Medinan verse. Whether this verse was "revealed" to Muḥammad while he was in Mecca, after his early arrival in Medina, or seventeen months after his call in Medina, these differing time frames become unimportant if the ruling in Q 2.256 ("no compulsion in religion" principle) is ultimately abrogated, or superseded, by the Sword verse and other fighting verses.

Q 2.256 and Abrogation

Whether this verse was revealed for the specific case ("occasion") of the Medinan Jewish adoptees or the Muslim father al-Ḥuṣayn, what would preclude the general application of its ruling ("no compulsion in religion" principle)?

To determine if Q 2.256 is applicable today requires the review of scholarly opinion regarding this verse and its possible abrogation, or nullification. In this case, the Muslim scholars are divided, with one group stating that

Q 2.256 has been abrogated and the other group stating that its ruling remains intact but with certain conditions.

Those scholars who consider Q 2.256 an abrogated verse submit the following as the abrogating verses:[38]

- Q 9.5 (Sword verse): "*...slay the idolaters wherever you find them....*"

  In his commentary of Q 2.256, eminent Islamic scholar al-Baghawī remarks that this "no-compulsion" rule "was in the beginning before he [Muḥammad] was commanded to fight, so it became abrogated by the Sword verse."[39]
- Q 9.73 (a fighting verse): "*...struggle with the unbelievers and hypocrites....*"

However, al-Ṭabarī notes in his commentary that nearly all the scholars state that the People of the Book are not to be coerced to convert to Islam—but only if they pay a head tax (*jizya**).[40] Although this "no coercion" is conditional to the payment of a tribute, it does not apply to Arabs. The commentaries confirm that the **Arabs of the Arabian Peninsula have to either be killed or accept Islam**.[41]

The team of scholars who agree that Q 2.256 has not been abrogated also state that it means that the People of the Book will not be compelled to convert to Islam if they pay the tribute according to the command in Q 9.29: "*...until they pay the tribute out of hand and have been humbled.*"[42] However, those who are being compelled to convert to Islam and are adherents of other religions will receive harsher treatment, as commanded by Q 9.73 (Sale trans.): "O prophet, wage war against the unbelievers and the hypocrites, and be severe unto them...."[43]

In summary, the team that does not support the abrogation of this verse offers a mixed opinion:

- Q 2.256 is not abrogated concerning the People of the Book.
- Q 2.256 is abrogated in all other cases.

Still, the viewpoints of both teams of scholars do not reflect true religious tolerance. In one case, the People of the Book (Christians and Jews) are allowed to keep their religions, only to suffer financial and moral humiliation through the payment of taxes. In the second case, those who are not Christians and Jews must face war (death).

Some of those who consider Q 2.256 not abrogated state that its meaning concerns superficial faith, explaining that one cannot force another into deep faith, or "belief in the heart."[44] With this understanding, Muslims can still compel non-Muslims to convert to Islam even if they can only generate superficial, if not true, faith in their hearts.

However, the very principle of "no compulsion in religion" is abrogated, even for the People of the Book, when new rules are applied to this principle—in this case, the requirement of taxation to avoid forced conversion or death. Moreover, the spirit of Q 2.256 is abrogated by the practices of Muḥammad, the role model for Muslims. His rationale for his wars for the Islamization of Medina's perimeter and the seizure of Mecca, compelling all its Meccan people to convert to Islam, has become one of Islam's core beliefs. In this manner, Muḥammad's real-world practices concerning the issue of religious freedom indicate that Q 2.256 has been practically abrogated by his precedent, despite the philosophical differences about the verse's abrogation by the Islamic scholars.

Muslim scholar and commentator al-Qurṭubī summarizes the ruling in Q 2.256 in his commentary:[45]

1. **Q 2.256 has been abrogated** because Muḥammad "compelled the Arabs to embrace Islam and fought them and did not accept any alternative but their surrender to Islam." Furthermore, this verse has been abrogated by Q 9.73 (Sale trans.): "O prophet, wage war against the unbelievers and the hypocrites, and be severe unto them…."

2. **Q 2.256 has not been abrogated under special conditions.** It was revealed "especially concerning the People of the Book, as they cannot be compelled to embrace Islam if they pay the *jizya* (tribute). It is only the idol worshippers who are compelled to embrace Islam" or else they must be killed.

3. **Q 2.256 is specific to the occasion about the Muslim father al-Ḥuṣayn** (see Occasion A) whose sons converted to Christianity and migrated to the Levant.

4. **Q 2.256 is specific to the occasion about the Medinan Jewish adoptees** (see Occasion B2) and the verse was revealed in the time of the evacuation of Banū al-Naḍīr.

5. **Q 2.256 is limited to the adult captives of the People of the Book**, because they are not compelled to embrace Islam. But if the captives are "young or old infidels and magi, or idolaters, they are compelled to adopt Islam, because whoever captures them cannot exploit them while they are still idolaters." All these captives are like filth to the Muslim master: their sacrifices cannot be eaten and their women cannot be used for sexual purposes. However, he is "allowed to compel them [to convert to Islam]" and then he can exploit them.

6. **Q 2.256's phrase "no compulsion in religion"** (Pickthall trans.) **means that those who convert to Islam under the sword are not to be described as "forced or compelled."**

In all this discussion and commentary concerning the abrogation of Q 2.256, the final word was stated by Muḥammad near the end of his life, when he announced sura al-Tawba (Q 9), one of the last "revealed" chapters of the Qur'ān. This chapter contains the definitive opinion of Islam regarding religious freedom in two most noteworthy verses: Q 9.5, the Sword verse, and Q 9.73, one of the fighting verses. However, the Sword verse is more formidable, abrogating at least 114 verses,[46] with these merciless, ruthless words: "*...slay the idolaters wherever you find them, and take them, and confine them, and lie in wait for them at every place of ambush....*" (Arberry trans.) (See the table "Qur'ānic Verses Abrogated by the Sword Verse," page 55.)

Explanation of the Sword Verse

The growing change of early Islam's attitude and actions—from tolerance to violence toward non-Muslims—makes it clearly evident that the Sword verse (Q 9.5) has been invoked to abrogate a large number of earlier "revealed" pacifist verses.

As the overriding, authoritative verse, what legislation has the Sword verse prescribed? Muslim commentators throughout the centuries have presented their explanations:

1. **Killing infidels mandatory** (*"slay the idolaters"*)

Al-Qurṭubī clearly explains this meaning by discussing how Muḥammad's two closest Companions (and later, the first and fourth caliphs, respectively, after Muḥammad's death) Abū Bakr and 'Alī Ibn Abī Ṭālib applied the Sword verse:[47]

> It is allowed to kill them in any way, but some accounts forbid mutilation. However, when he [Abū Bakr] killed the people of apostasy, incinerating them with fire, stoning them, throwing them off the tops of the mountains, and hanging them in wells, perhaps he [Abū Bakr] acted on the general ruling of the verse. Also, when 'Alī burnt people of apostasy, he could have acted under the same understanding, based on the general context in the verse.

Some scholars state that the part *"slay the idolaters"* is abrogated by Q 47.4: *"...then set them free, either by grace or ransom...."* This verse (Q 47.4) commands mercy for captives, by either releasing them or accepting a ransom from them. However, according to al-Qurṭubī, the Sword verse abrogates Q 47.4: "It is not permissible for captive idolaters [to receive any other treatment] except to be killed."[47]

Despite the differing opinions on this issue, notice that the text regarding the acceptance of ransom is conditional.[49] Before the Muslims take enemy captives, they must first cause rivers of blood, according to the first part of Q 47.4: *"When you meet the unbelievers, smite their necks, then, when you have made wide slaughter among them, tie fast the bonds...."*

2. **Killing infidels immediately** (*"wherever you find them"*)
   Al-Ṭabarī states that this phrase means any Muslim who encounters an infidel, no matter the place or time, must kill the infidel without any consideration to the sanctity of the infidel's surroundings,[50] i.e., sacred places.

   The Shiite commentator al-Ṭabāṭabā'ī explains that the purpose of the verse's command—to kill the infidels wherever found—is to exterminate them and rid the world of them in order to "save the people from contact or relationships with infidels."[51] According to this explanation, the world cannot be "clean" until all non-Muslims are eradicated.

3. **Capturing infidels** (*"and take them"*)
   Al-Ṭabarī states that this part of the verse commands the taking of infidels as captives.[52] However, Muḥammad 'Abdu* (AD 1849-1905), the renowned Egyptian Islamic jurist, religious scholar and liberal reformer, warns that taking captives is conditional, according to Q 8.67 (Sale trans.): "It hath not been [granted] unto any prophet, that he should possess captives, until he had made a great slaughter [of the infidels] in the earth...."[53] According to this Islamist modernist, Islam does not allow the taking of captives prior to the subjugation of the enemy through widespread slaughter. Thus, the relationship here regarding killing and capturing is not about selecting or abrogating one action over the other; rather, the two approaches are integrated, with the attacking and killing first of infidels, followed by the capture of any survivors.

4. **Surrounding infidels** (*"and confine them"*)

   Muslim Shiite scholar Ṭabarsī (d. AD 1153) states that Muslims must block the way of infidels and besiege (*"confine"*) them. Ṭabarsī notes that, in general, the actions of killing, capturing, or besieging infidels should not be viewed as options in a prescribed order. Rather, the "evaluation of the situation will determine which action to select."[54]

   Muḥammad 'Abdu, the supposedly "enlightened" Muslim religious reformer, adds supportive commentary on this point by describing how to properly execute the besiegement of infidels:[55]

   > To besiege is to imprison and surround the enemy wherever they may be found, be it a stronghold or a fort, by prohibiting them from going out in chaos; but, if by attacking them a great loss is going to happen, then surround them until they surrender and follow your rule, with a condition that is acceptable by you or without a condition.

5. **Surveilling infidels everywhere** (*"and lie in wait for them at every place of ambush"*)

   Al-Qurṭubī explains that the *"place of ambush"* is the "place where the enemy is being observed" and that "it is permissible to assassinate them [infidels] before inviting them [to Islam]."[56] In other words, the Muslim fighter must lurk around infidels in order to kill or capture them.[57] In order to illustrate the scope and confining nature of the surveillance required from Muslims, a scholar clarifies this point: "Sit by every road they [infidels] take to their homes or their work."[58]

6. **Setting conditions for infidels** (*"But if they repent, and perform the prayer"*)
   Al-Ṭabarī states that repentance is rejecting polytheism for monotheism and accepting the prophethood of Muḥammad.[59] However, it is not sufficient for polytheists to declare their submission and acceptance of Islam; they must also perform the necessary rituals, e.g., prayer, almsgiving, etc., in apparent obedience.[60] Only after these idolaters prove their conversion through their words and actions will they be permitted by Muslims to *"go their way"* in safety and peace.

Escalation of Islam's Violence

Some Muslim commentators and scholars believe that the Sword verse does not actually abrogate the so-called 114 pacifist verses. According to Muḥammad 'Abdu, the Sword verse directive can be deferred, and he explains the purpose for postponing fighting:[61]

> What was delayed was the command to fight until the Muslims become stronger, **and in case of weakness, the provision is to tolerate harm with patience**...those commands [engage in peace or fighting] that have been revealed must be obeyed at some point for a certain situation that requires such provision; however, when that reason or situation changes, then follow the second command. This is not an abrogation, because abrogation is a removal of the provision [which means] it cannot be followed. (emphasis added)

So, given 'Abdu's explanation, the ruling in the Sword verse ("*...slay the idolaters...*") remains firm but its application can be flexible in terms of timing and context. According to 'Abdu, there is no objection to tactically returning to the principle of forgiveness until Muslims become stronger, if the circumstances are not favorable and Muslims are weak.

Sayīd Quṭb* (AD 1906-1966), Egyptian Islamic author and educator whose writings have become the theoretical foundation for many of today's "moderate" and radical Islamic groups, concurs with the temporary suspension of verse rulings. Quṭb states that the early Meccan texts can still be employed as long as they exist in the Qur'ān:[62]

> ...they [pacifist verses] remain to face similar situations and cases that have already been faced, but this does not restrict Muslims if they encounter situations **such as those encountered by the later texts** [Sword and fighting verses]**, especially if they are able to implement it.** (emphasis added)

Additionally, Quṭb strongly warns that it is wrong to believe that Islam is a religion of peace: "[I]t is only concerned about the peace within the borders of Islam only!"[63] He explains his position in clear terms:[64]

> **The absolute right of Islam** is to be released on earth to liberate humankind from enslavement of the slaves wherever feasible, to bring them back to only Allah, **regardless of whether there was an attack on its people inside their regional borders or not**[**!**] ...[This right] is the principle underlying jihad in Islam, and without it [jihad] the religion of Allah loses the right to remove the physical obstacles standing in the way of its call [Da'wa], and it [Islam] also loses its momentum and realism in facing the human reality..., [when it can only] **face material forces with** [just] **the Islamic call...a weakness that does not satisfy Allah for his religion on this earth.** (emphasis added)

This viewpoint of Quṭb, a significant Muslim Sunni scholar, is not isolated but is also espoused by the well-known Shiite reference Muḥammad Ḥusayn Faḍlāllah* (AD 1935-2010). Though considered a moderate Islamic thinker, he states that killing "the '*idolaters wherever you find them*' comes after arguing with them and after the warning time is over, without [the infidels] returning to the truth and righteousness."[65] Faḍlāllah further explains the meaning of "*take them, and confine them, and lie in wait for them*":[66]

> It [the taking, beseiging, and surveillance of idolaters] seems to denote the closure of the roads and besieging them from every corner. In this case, **the issue is no longer a case of making choices between killing or imprisoning them**, as it was said; **it is the issue of killing whoever is found without compunction and the issue of pursuing whoever has fled or disappeared, so that the punishment of Allah takes place after he is taken and beseiged.** (emphasis added)

Given these detailed explanations by Faḍlāllah and ʿAbdu (considered moderate Islamic scholars and commentators), and Quṭb regarding the Sword verse and abrogation, the consensus opinion here is that though the Sword verse does not abrogate the earlier Meccan pacifist verses, the directive in the Sword verse—the killing of infidels—is also not removed. The only "moderation" presented by these scholars is the timing and the circumstances for this violence.

Sword Verse Abrogations

According to Islamic scholar Ibn al-Jawzī (AH 508-597/ AD 1114-1200), sura al-Tawba (Q 9) abrogates every earlier instruction to Muḥammad to turn away from those who do not accept Islam and wait instead for Allah to decide the fate of those who would reject Muḥammad's call.[67] This sura includes the Sword verse (Q 9.5), which declares and highlights the principle of jihad, the organizing principle regarding the relationship of Muslims with others. The Sword verse also abrogates the "verses of tolerance and treaty, and the [Sword] verse applies to all infidels everywhere."[68] (For a list of the commonly acknowledged abrogated verses, see the table "Qur'ānic Verses Abrogated by the Sword Verse," page 55.)

To better understand the sweep of this abrogation, the following list categorizes major principles with the corresponding verses abrogated by the Sword verse:

1. **Sword verse abrogates the peaceful approach of the call, thus cancelling the following principles or rulings "revealed" in these earlier verses:**

   - Muḥammad—a messenger only
     Q 3.20: "*...it is only to deliver the Message....*"
     Q 5.99: "*It is only for the Messenger to deliver the Message....*"
     Q 11.12: "*...Thou art only a warner....*"
   - Kind approach of call
     Q 2.83: "*...and speak good to men....*"
     Q 16.125: "*Call thou to the way of thy Lord with wisdom and good admonition, and dispute with them in the better way....*"
   - Patience and forgiveness of rejecters
     Q 15.85: "*...so pardon thou, with a gracious pardoning.*"
     Q 25.63: "*...when the ignorant address them, say, 'Peace'.*"

   The Sword verse also abrogates the directive addressed to Muḥammad in Q 20.130 ("*So be thou patient under what they say...*"), counseling him to endure the rebuff of those who reject his message and to overlook their accusations, indicting him of being a magician, madman, and poet.[69]

   The Sword verse also abrogates Muḥammad's requirement in Q 41.34 ("*Not equal are the good deed and the evil deed. Repel with that which is fairer...*"), charging Muḥammad to respond to insults with goodly, respectful behavior.

2. **Sword verse abrogates the principle of religious freedom, thus cancelling the following principles or rulings "revealed" in these earlier verses:**

    - Freedom of people to keep their own religion
      Q 2.256: *"No compulsion is there in religion...."*
      Q 109.6: *"To you your religion, and to me my religion!"*
      Q 2.139: *"...Our deeds belong to us, and to you belong your deeds...."*

    - Freedom to accept or reject Islam
      Q 6.104: *"...Whoso sees clearly, it is to his own gain, and whoso is blind, it is to his own loss; I am not a watcher over you...."* (This verse declares that faith in Islam is left to individual choice.)
      Q 10.99: *"...Wouldst thou then constrain the people, until they are believers?"* (Muḥammad's directive here is to deliver the message of Islam but not force people to convert.)

3. **Sword verse abrogates the principle of tolerance with non-Muslims, thus cancelling the following principles or rulings "revealed" in these earlier verses:**

    - Tolerance with those who refuse to accept Islam
      Q 5.105: *"O believers, look after your own souls. He who is astray cannot hurt you, if you are rightly guided...."* (This verse supports the principle of religious freedom for those who do not believe in Islam.)
      Q 6.106: *"...and turn thou away from the idolaters."*

    - Tolerance for the People of the Book
      Q 2.109: *"...yet do you pardon and be forgiving, till God brings His command...."* (This verse asks for pardon and forgiveness to those who argue with Muslims about religion. Al-Zamakhsharī states that this verse refers to the Jews.)[70]

4. **Sword verse abrogates the principle of peace, thus cancelling the following principles or rulings "revealed" in these earlier verses:**

   - Defensive wars only
     Q 2.190: *"And fight in the way of God with those; who fight with you, but aggress not...."* (With the abrogation of this provision, the purpose of the war switches from defense to offense.)
   - Respect for truce proposals
     Q 8.61: *"And if they incline to peace, do thou incline to it...."*
     Q 2.192: *"but if they give over, surely God is All-forgiving, All-compassionate."* (Some opinions state that the meaning here is to "give over," or desist from killing Muslims.)[71]
   - Adherence to covenants made with enemies
     Q 4.90: *"...If they withdraw from you, and do not fight you, and offer you peace, then God assigns not any way to you against them."* (Even though the Qur'ān allows Muslims to make peace covenants and conventions with others in this verse, the same Qur'ān through the Sword verse invalidates all previous peace covenants.)

Final Comments

Two points regarding the far-reaching impact of the Sword verse necessitate greater discussion:

- Abrogation of the principle of wars for defense purposes only to wars of aggression
- Definition of "idolaters" in the Sword verse (essentially, the Qur'ānic perception)

Abrogation of Defensive War Principle

The consensus of Muslim scholars firmly states that Q 2.190 (*"And fight in the way of God with those who fight with you, but aggress not: God loves not the aggressors"*), the verse about war for defensive purposes only, has been abrogated by the Sword and other fighting verses. This abrogation occurs on two levels because the verse contains two parts:

- **Part One:** *"And fight in the way of God with those who fight with you..."*
- **Part Two:** *"...but aggress not...."*

Part One of this verse allows fighting only if first attacked, which means that Muslims should not fight if they are not being attacked. However, Part One has been abrogated by verses that directly command aggressive action:[72]

- Q 2.191: *"And slay them wherever you come upon them...."* (See also Q 4.91.)
- Q 9.5: *"...slay the idolaters wherever you find them...."*
- Q 9.29: *"Fight those who believe not in God and the Last Day...."*
- Q 9.36: *"...And fight the unbelievers totally even as they fight you totally...."*

Thus, the Muslims are no longer commanded to defend themselves only; rather they should wage war on all infidels (Q 9.29) and kill them wherever possible (Q 2.191, Q 9.5). Anyone who does not believe in Islam is thus considered an enemy of Muslims, regardless of his or her religion (Q 9.36).

In Part Two of this verse ("*...but aggress not...*"), the Muslim scholars state that the assault or fighting excludes the killing of women and children, initiating a fight without provocation, and attacking during the sacred months.[73] However, the following fighting verses abrogate Part Two of the verse, according to other scholars:[74]

- Q 9.36: "*...And fight the unbelievers totally even as they fight you totally....*"
- Q 9.5: "*...slay the idolaters wherever you find them....*"

Therefore, the entire abrogation of Q 2.190, Parts One and Two, means that war can be conducted not only for aggressive purposes but also for extermination—the killing of all individuals—which thus permits the killing of women and children. The purpose of war then becomes all-encompassing with the extermination of the enemy its goal.

Qur'ānic Definition of "Idolaters"

The Sword verse targets "idolaters": "*...slay the idolaters wherever you find them....*" Who are these "idolaters"? Some may respond that this term refers only to polytheists and does not include the People of the Book, the Qur'ān's name or label for Christians and Jews. However, the Qur'ānic concept of polytheists applies even to Christians and Jews, based on the following verses:

- Q 9.30: *"The Jews say, 'Ezra is the Son of God'; the Christians say, 'The Messiah is the Son of God'...conforming with the unbelievers before them. God assail them! How they are perverted!"*
- Q 9.31: *"They have taken their* [Jewish] *rabbis and their* [Christian] *monks as lords apart from God, and the Messiah, Mary's son—and they were commanded to serve but One God...."*

In his explanation of Q 9.31, Muslim commentator and historian Ibn Kathīr (AH 701-774/AD 1301-1373) notes that the Qur'ān considers Jews and Christians to be polytheists, and that the Qur'ān incites Muslims to fight them, stating, "This [Qur'ānic incitement] is an inducement from Allah almighty for the faithful to fight the **infidel polytheists, the Jews and Christians**, for saying such fabricated heinous lies about Allah" (emphasis added).[75]

Charging Jews and Christians of polytheism is expressed in other verses of the Qur'ān, such as the following passage (Hilâlî-Khân trans. Q 4.47-48):

> O you who have been given the Scripture (Jews and Christians)! Believe in what We have revealed (to Muḥammad…) confirming what is (already) with you, before We efface faces (by making them like the back of necks; without nose, mouth, eyes, etc.) and turn them hindwards, or curse them as We cursed the Sabbathbreakers. And the Commandment of Allah is always executed. / Verily, Allah forgives not that partners should be set up with him in worship,…and whoever sets up partners with Allah in worship, he has indeed invented a tremendous sin.

According to al-Ṭabarī, these condemning verses are directed toward the "People of the Book."[76] In yet other verses, the Qur'ān accuses Christians of denying the oneness of God and worshipping three gods: *"They are unbelievers who say, 'God is the Third of Three.' No god is there but One God…"* (Arberry trans. Q 5.73; compare with Q 4.171). Therefore, in the Qur'ān the term "polytheism" includes the pagan religions as well as Judaism and Christianity that existed in the Arabian Peninsula during Muḥammad's time.

"Idolater": Definition with Consequences

Yet Islam is not satisfied with just classifying non-Muslims as "infidels" or "idolaters" but commands its followers to treat these non-Muslims differently, exceeding mere definition with action.

In one verse, Q 9.28, polytheists are described as unclean: *"O believers, the idolaters are indeed unclean…."* With this statement, the "idolaters"—polytheists—are classified as "unclean," which means here spiritually impure.

Because Jews and Christians are considered polytheists (review Q 9.31), the logical assumption here is that the description of "unclean" is not limited to the followers of the nonbiblical religions but also applies to the People of the Book—in other words, Jews and Christians. Based on this interpretation, Muslim jurisprudents state that the People of the Book "are unclean persons and should be avoided."[77] Al-Ḥasan Ibn 'Alī (son of 'Alī Ibn Abī Ṭālib and grandson of Muḥammad) states that "whoever shakes hands with a polytheist must perform ablution."[78]

However, the Ḥadīth literature reports that Muḥammad desired more than avoidance and ablution when dealing with non-Muslims. He wanted their expulsion from the Arabian Peninsula:

> ...The Prophet on his deathbed, gave three orders saying, "Expel the pagans [polytheists] from the Arabian Peninsula, respect and give gifts to the foreign delegates as you have seen me dealing with them." I [Ibn 'Abbas] forgot the third (order). (Ya'qub bin Muḥammad said, "I asked Al-Mughira bin 'Abdur-Raḥman about the Arabian Peninsula and he said, 'It comprises Mecca, Medina, Al-Yama-ma and Yemen." Ya'qub added, "And Al-Arj, the beginning of Tihama.")[79]

> Malik said that Ibn Shihab said, "'Umar Ibn al-Khattab searched for information until he was absolutely convinced that the Messenger of Allah... had said, 'No two *deens* [religions] shall coexist in the Arabian Peninsula.' He [Umar Ibn al-Khattab] therefore expelled the Jews from Khaybar."[80]

These *ḥadīth* reports, Muḥammad's evacuation of the Banū al-Naḍīr Jews (and eventually all Jews from Medina), and the Qur'ān (see Q 59) have thus been used to justify the practice of expelling non-Muslims, including the People of the Book, in all Islamic countries since Muḥammad's death.

Today's so-called moderate Islamic scholars, such as Lebanon's Grand Mufti Ḥasan Khāled (AD 1921-1989), hold an even stronger position, expressing that for all idolaters and those who take false gods other than Allah, the "Islam position of this [worship] is war without any mercy."[81] And this position perfectly aligns with the directive in the Sword verse, "*…slay the idolaters wherever you find them….*"

Conclusion

Muḥammad arrived to Medina in AD 622 because his call of thirteen years in Mecca had proved futile, as the majority of his own people, the Meccans, still resolutely continued to follow their own beliefs. Thus Muḥammad entered Medina with only a very small number of followers. Into this new city, he carried with him not only a great moral defeat after failing to convert Mecca to Islam but the tormented memories of his Quraysh tribesmen's disdain of him and his "Qur'ān."

In Medina, his small band of followers struggled to establish a livelihood or collect a pension, as the doors to local trade were not available or accessible to them. These difficulties prompted their decision to embark on raids, using the plunder as their means of financial support. The

Qur'ān recognizes implicitly that the campaigns of the Muslims were designed to collect booty: *"The Bedouins who were left behind will say, when you set forth after spoils, to take them, 'Let us follow you'…"* (Q 48.15). Thus, the Qur'ān confirms that the Muslims began their early battles for the collection of financial resources.

At the end of his life, Muḥammad announced sura Tawba (Q 9), which contains the Sword verse (Q 9.5), where the Qur'ān orders fighting. According to Muḥammad Muṣṭafā al-Marāghī, an Egyptian reformist Islamic scholar (AD 1881-1945), this fighting "was postponed until the Muslims become stronger and **in case of weakness, the provision is to tolerate harm with patience**" (emphasis added).[82]

Quṭb, in his commentary of Q 8.61 (*"And if they incline to peace, do thou incline to it; and put thy trust in God…"*), maintains that the directive to Muḥammad in Q 8.61 was only meant to be temporary, its authority overridden by the later Sword and fighting verses in Q 9:[83]

> [This verse Q 8.61] does not contain an absolute definitive rule in this matter and that the final rules are revealed later in sura Tawba [Q 9]. However, Allah commanded his messenger [Muḥammad] to accept being in peace with the people that he had renounced and not fight them, whether or not he had a covenant with them at the time. And he continued to keep peace with others, infidels and the People of the Book, until the rules of sura Tawba were revealed. From that time on, nothing was accepted anymore but converting to Islam or paying *jizya*—**And this is the kind of acceptable peace** as long as those people obeyed their covenant [with Muḥammad]—**or else it would be fighting whenever Muslims can do it until the whole religion will be for Allah**.
>
> And I am giving more details in this matter to clarify the uncertainty stemming from the spiritual and mental defeat many people suffer today who are writing about jihad in Islam, where the pressure of the present reality is becoming heavy on their souls and minds....[T]hey think it [global holy war] is too much for their religion—when they don't realize its truth—to have a constant method, which is facing the whole humanity with one of the following three options: **Islam or *jizya* or fighting**....(emphasis added)

The three options—Islam, *jizya*, or fighting—that Quṭb insists is the "constant method" of Islam continue to reverberate in today's Muslim world. For instance, these same options were included in the ultimatum issued by Islamic State (ISIS or ISIL), when this jihadist insurgency group took over large areas in Iraq and war-torn Syria in 2014. Upon its forced control of Mosul, a northern city in Iraq, its leadership announced that resident Christians had three choices: "Islam; the dhimma contract—involving payment of jizya; if they [Christians] refuse this they will have nothing but the sword."[84]

So, according to Quṭb and those who agree with his opinion, there is no lasting conflict between the pacifist and the fighting verses. The directives in the later revealed verses of sura Tawba (Q 9) take precedence and should be the priority of all dedicated Muslims.

The conflict in Stevenson's novel also ends—with the death of the split-personality protagonist. Dr. Jekyll transforms into Mr. Hyde, the evil personality, who then commits suicide; his death is the conclusion of this story.

However, the Qur'ān's "Mr. Hyde" (Sword and other fighting verses) conquers "Dr. Jekyll" (pacifist verses). Its text is divided, having a character with two spirits, two faces, and two hearts. However, these two opposing sides are not equal in power: As is revealed, the master and leading spirit is the Sword verse and its siblings, the various fighting verses. Yet, Muslims continue to selectively present and highlight the Qur'ān's pacifist verses in the West and at international organizations.

But this deception is nothing but the smart propaganda of mummified text, artful masks covering the active living monster in the Sword verse.

Resources and References

This section contains important resources as well as traditional references to assist the reader in understanding the information presented in this book. All these materials will better familiarize the reader with the concepts related to the Sword verse, help the reader in topic searches and relevant information, and enhance the reader's knowledge and understanding concerning the text and subsequent impact of the Sword verse.

Qur'ānic Verses Abrogated by the Sword Verse

This table presents the majority of the verses that Islamic scholars have determined abrogated by the Sword verse, Q 9.5. The selected verses are organized in numerical (rather than revelatory) order, and each verse includes a sample reference list of Islamic scholars who support its abrogation as well as an abbreviated commentary to explain the scholars' opinion.

Sword Verse Table Index

This index is especially designed for use with the preceding table. Readers can search verses abrogated by the Sword verse by topic. In this way, readers can more quickly understand the kinds of issues addressed and abrogated in these verses, the frequency of certain abrogations, and the kinds of people impacted by these abrogations.

Special Names and Terms

This section contains additional information about individuals or complex terms mentioned in this book that require further explanation to enhance reader understanding.

Endnotes

Because of the extensive research contained in this book, endnotes (rather than parenthetical documentation) were used to cite the textual references to better maintain content flow and ease of readability.

Bibliography

All Arabic and English sources cited in this book are listed together alphabetically by last name in this section. The type of media—print or Web—is indicated with each source.

Name Index

Names of people and spiritual beings are listed alphabetically in the book. For best identification and access, the names are those persons who lived centuries ago are alphabetized by their first or most well-known name; contemporary names are listed alphabetically by last name.

Subject Index

Major topics discussed in this book are alphabetically arranged and linked with corresponding page numbers to enhance and expedite reader access to the content.

Qur'ānic Verses Abrogated by the Sword Verse

Arberry English Translation (unless otherwise noted)

This Sword verse table presents the majority of the verses that Islamic scholars have determined abrogated by the Sword verse Q 9.5. Most Islamic scholars have determined that the number of verses abrogated by the Sword verse is 114 (see al-Zarkashī 2: 40) or 124 (see Ibn Salāma 51). As these different listings do not coincide, the list presented in this table is longer than either of these two lists, because it contains some abrogated verses that are only found in one but not both types of listings.

Some verses were excluded from this table because the commentators' reasons for their abrogation are weak, unconvincing, or contradictory. For example, some commentators (see Ibn Salāma 101) state that Q 95.8 (*"Is not God the justest of judges?"*) has been abrogated. However, to abrogate this verse would mean that God is not the most just of judges, which directly conflicts with the most basic Islamic doctrine concerning the unity and supremacy of God; the Sword verse cannot be applied to this verse, because it cannot abrogate the Muslim belief that Allah is the wisest, the best of judges.

NOTE: Boldfaced text indicates the abrogated part of each verse.

1 Q 2.83
*...**and speak good to men**....*

Commentary: A team of scholars views this verse as a call for peace, because it urges Muslims to speak kindly to the Jews. Therefore, they state that this verse is abrogated, because every call for peace is abrogated and specifically abrogated by the Sword verse (al-Makkī 124; Ibn Ḥazm 21; al-Naḥḥās 1: 509).

2 Q 2.109
Many of the People of the Book wish they might restore you as unbelievers, after you have believed, in the jealousy of their souls, after the truth has become clear to them; ***yet do you pardon and be forgiving, till God brings His command****;....*

Commentary: Though this verse states that Jews and Christians, from selfish envy, would gladly like to see Muslims return to unbelief, it urges Muslims to forgive them. However, this call for forbearance has been abrogated by the Sword verse (Ibn al-Jawzī, *Nawāsikh* 136-137).

NOTE: When Islam hardened its position toward the People of the Book, the Sword verse became the primary instrument for nullifying the earlier Meccan verses that urged tolerance toward the People of the Book.

3 Q 2.139
Say: 'Would you then dispute with us concerning God, who is our Lord and your Lord? ***Our deeds belong to us, and to you belong your deeds****; Him we serve sincerely.'*

Commentary: A team of scholars states that this verse advocates religious tolerance toward Jews and Christians, and so this verse is abrogated by the Sword verse (Ibn Salāma 14).

4a Q 2.190
And fight in the way of God with those who fight with you...

Commentary: The beginning phrase of the verse (*"And fight in God's way with those who fight with you"*) requires fighting only if a polytheist initiates the fight; unless attacked, the Muslim should not initiate a fight. This provision has been abrogated by the Sword verse (Ibn al-Jawzī, *Nawāsikh* 179).

4b Q 2.190
...but aggress not: God loves not the aggressors.

Commentary: The term *"aggress not"* refers to the (a) killing of women and children, (b) initiating of fights, and (c) initiating of fights during sacred months. However, this principle of "aggress not" is abrogated by the Sword verse (Ibn Salāma 19; al-Makkī 155-156; Ibn al-Jawzī, *Nawāsikh* 180).

NOTE: With this abrogation by the Sword verse, it is therefore the right of Muslims to initiate fighting, even during the Arabs' sacred months when violence is generally prohibited. However, the danger in abrogating the principle of "aggress not" by the Sword verse means that the prohibition of killing women and children may not be honored.

5 Q 2.191
And slay them wherever you come upon them, and expel them from where they expelled you; persecution is more grievous than slaying. ***But fight them not by the Holy Mosque until they should fight you there; then, if they fight you, slay them****—such is the recompense of unbelievers.*

Commentary: The verse prevents fighting the enemy in the area of the Grand Mosque, unless the fighting is initiated by the enemy. But this prohibition is abrogated by the Sword verse, which allows fighting in every time and place (Ibn Salāma 19; al-Naḥḥās 1: 521; Ibn al-Jawzī, *Nawāsikh* 181-182).

6 Q 2.192
but if they give over, surely God is All-forgiving, All-compassionate.

Commentary: Some scholars state that the prohibition is about fighting those polytheists who stop fighting; the verse's meaning is about conciliation, pardon and mercy. However, this tolerance is abrogated by the Sword verse (Ibn Salāma 19; Ibn al-Jawzī, *Nawāsikh* 185; Ibn Ḥazm 27).

7 Q 2.217
They will question thee concerning the holy month, and fighting in it. Say: 'Fighting in it is a heinous thing, *but to bar from God's way, and disbelief in Him…is more heinous in God's sight….*

NOTE: Muḥammad sent out a reconnaissance brigade, led by 'Abd Allāh Ibn Jaḥsh, but the brigade instead raided a Quraysh commercial convoy during Rajab, a sacred month for the Arabs. (In describing the inviolate nature of these special months, the Arab pagans would state that if a man passed by the murderer of his father during a sacred month, "he wouldn't wake him up.") Some Quraysh escorts were killed during this raid, an act that disturbed some Muslims. Thus, this verse came to defend the killings committed by Ibn Jaḥsh's brigade. (See also the section Medinan Period (AH 1-11/AD 622-632), page 11.)

Commentary: Though the verse recognizes the sanctity of this month, it justifies the breach of this sanctity by implying that the Quraysh must bear the responsibility (and blame) for forcing Muslims to leave Mecca (*"but to bar from God's way, and disbelief in Him…is more heinous in God's sight…"*).

Later, the Muslims considered that no circumstance or place is forbidden from fighting; therefore, according to all Islamic commentators, this verse is considered abrogated. According to various opinions, it is abrogated by the Sword verse (al-Naḥḥās 1: 536; Ibn al-Jawzī, *Nawāsikh* 197; al-Makkī 160; Ibn Ḥazm 28).

8 Q 2.256
No compulsion is there in religion....

Commentary: In this verse, Muḥammad declares that people have the right to keep their own religion, and that it is not permissible to compel anyone to embrace Islam. However, this forthright declaration for personal religious freedom has been abrogated by the Sword verse (Ibn Salāma 27; Ibn al-Jawzī, *Nawāsikh* 219; see also Baghawī 1: 314 and al-Qurṭubī 4: 280).

NOTE: Interestingly, the occasion (or historical circumstances) for this sweeping announcement is not definitive, as there are several variations to the story context about this verse. (See the section Challenges to the Sword Verse, page 21.)

9 Q 3.20
...And say to those who have been given the Book and to the common folk: 'Have you surrendered?' If they have surrendered, they are right guided; ***but if they turn their backs, thine it is only to deliver the Message****; and God sees His servants.*

Commentary: According to this section of the verse, Muḥammad's responsibility is only to convey Allah's message. A group of Muslim scholars state that this limited role is abrogated by the Sword verse (Ibn Salāma 29; Ibn al-Jawzī, *Nawāsikh* 237; Ibn Ḥazm 30).

10 Q 3.28
Let not the believers take the unbelievers for friends, rather than the believers—for whoso does that belongs not to God in anything— ***unless you have a fear of them....***

Commentary: One team of scholars states that the verse is telling Muslims to avoid polytheists, unless they fear danger from the polytheists if they don't associate with them. However, this directive for avoidance is abrogated by the Sword verse. Another scholar clarifies that the permissibility of avoidance resulted from the Muslims' weakness in the early stages of Islam, but this directive for avoidance was abrogated as soon as Islam became stronger (Ibn Salāma 29; Ibn al-Jawzī, *Nawāsikh* 238; Shu'la 120).

11 Q 3.186

…and you shall hear from those who were given the Book before you, and from those who are idolaters, much hurt; ***but if you are patient and godfearing—surely that is true constancy.***

Commentary: A team of scholars states that the patience mentioned in this verse is abrogated by the Sword verse (Ibn al-Jawzī, *Nawāsikh* 246).

12 Q 4.63

Those—God knows what is in their hearts; ***so turn away from them, and admonish them, and say to them penetrating words about themselves.***

Commentary: This verse directs Muḥammad to ignore, enlighten, and advise his critics to save their souls; this response is all he can do, but Allah knows their innermost intentions. However, this directive to counter harsh criticism with a passive, verbal response has been abrogated by the Sword verse (Ibn Salāma 37; Ibn al-Jawzī, *Nawāsikh* 281; Shu'la 127; al-Makkī 252; Ibn Ḥazm 34).

NOTE: The principle of preaching and turning away from his critics was only applied at the beginning of Muḥammad's call. When the Muslims became stronger after the Hijra, Muḥammad's peaceful verbal response to his opposition transformed into a violent, physical one.

13 Q 4.80

Whosoever obeys the Messenger, thereby obeys God; ***and whosoever turns his back—We have not sent thee to be a watcher over them.***

Commentary: Even though this verse tells Muslims to obey Muḥammad, it stresses that Muḥammad is not their guardian. However, this limited role for Muḥammad is abrogated by the Sword verse (Ibn Salāma 38; Ibn al-Jawzī, *Nawāsikh* 284; Ibn Ḥazm 34).

14 Q 4.81

They say, 'Obedience'; but when they sally [go] forth from thee, a party of them meditate all night on other than what thou sayest. God writes down their meditations; ***so turn away from them,*** *and put thy trust in God; God suffices for a guardian.*

Commentary: This verse commands Muḥammad not to concern himself with those who show faith but later scheme against Muḥammad's words. Some commentators state that the verse means Muḥammad should avoid these insincere believers, or hypocrites. However, the verse's directive to Muḥammad to forgive these hypocritical Muslims is abrogated by the Sword verse (Ibn Salāma 38; Ibn al-Jawzī, *Nawāsikh* 284; Ibn Ḥazm 34).

15 Q 4.84

So do thou fight in the way of God; thou art charged only with thyself....

Commentary: One team of scholars states that the verse requires Muḥammad to fight for Allah's cause and may urge other Muslim believers, but he is not to impose this duty of war on others. Commentators state that this restriction is abrogated by the Sword verse (Ibn Salāma 38; Ibn al-Jawzī, *Nawāsikh* 284; Ibn Ḥazm 35; see also al-Zamakhsharī 2: 117-118).

16a Q 4.90

except those that betake themselves to a people who are joined with you by a compact,...

Commentary: This verse permits Muslims to maintain peace and conventions with allies. But the Qur'ān has invalidated all conventions for peace, so this principle for honoring treaties with non-Muslims is abrogated by the Sword verse (Ibn Salāma 38; al-Naḥḥās 2: 213; al-Makkī 230; Ibn al-Jawzī, *Nawāsikh* 285-286).

16b Q 4.90

...or come to you with breasts constricted from fighting with you or fighting their people. Had God willed, He would have given them authority over you, and then certainly they would have fought you. If they withdraw from you, and do not fight you, and offer you peace, then God assigns not any way to you against them.

Commentary: The verse commands Muslims not to fight enemies who have stopped fighting and wish to reconcile, and it commands them to accept the reconciliation. However, this principle is abrogated by the Sword verse (Ibn Salāma 38; al-Makkī 231; Ibn al-Jawzī, *Nawāsikh* 285-286).

17 Q 4.91

You will find others desiring to be secure from you, and secure from their people....

Commentary: This verse tells Muslims that when they encounter people who wish to remain neutral in order to protect themselves from Muslims and enemies of Muslims, Muslims are to grant peace to the neutral party. However, this peaceful accord with neutral parties is abrogated by the Sword verse (Ibn Salāma 38; Ibn al-Jawzī, *Nawāsikh* 287; Ibn Ḥazm 34-35).

18 Q 4.92

It is not for a believer to kill a believer except (that it be) by mistake, and whosoever kills a believer by mistake, (it is ordained that) he must set free a believing slave and a compensation (blood money, i.e. Diya) be given to the deceased's family, unless they remit it. If the deceased belonged to a people at war with you and he was a believer; the freeing of a believing slave (is prescribed), and **if he belonged to a people with whom you have a treaty of mutual alliance, compensation (blood money - Diya) must be paid to his family**, and a believing slave must be freed. And whoso finds this (the penance of freeing a slave) beyond his means, he must fast for two consecutive months in order to seek repentance from Allah. And Allah is Ever All-Knowing, All-Wise. (Hilâlî-Khan trâns.)

Commentary: Some exegetes of the Qur'ān state that the verse refers to the polytheists who had an alliance and truce with Muḥammad for a certain earlier period of time. Therefore, this earlier relationship is abrogated by the Sword verse (al-Makkī 231-232).

19 Q 5.2

O believers, profane not God's waymarks nor the holy month, neither the offering, nor the necklaces, ***nor those repairing to the Holy House seeking from their Lord bounty and good pleasure****....*

Commentary: This verse prohibits Muslims from obstructing polytheists on their pilgrimages to Mecca. But this prohibition has been abrogated by the Sword verse (Ibn Salāma 40; al-Naḥḥās 2: 235; Ibn al-Jawzī, *Nawāsikh* 298-299; al-Makkī 256).

20 Q 5.13

So for their breaking their compact We cursed them and made their hearts hard, they perverting words from their meanings; and they have forgotten a portion of that they were reminded of; and thou wilt never cease to light upon some act of treachery on their part, except a few of them. ***Yet pardon them, and forgive****; surely God loves the good-doers.*

Commentary: According to Islamic sources, the verse relates to an allegation that a group of Jews plotted against Muḥammad. These sources mention that the verse gives Muḥammad the right to pardon them because of the treaty between Muḥammad and the Jews. However, some scholars consider this "pardon" abrogated by the Sword verse (Ibn al-Jawzī, *Nawāsikh* 308; al-Makkī 269).

21 Q 5.99

It is only for the Messenger to deliver the Message*; and God knows what you reveal and what you hide.*

Commentary: The verse states that the mission of Muḥammad is to only deliver Allah's message, but a team of scholars states that this verse is abrogated by the Sword verse (Ibn Salāma 42; Ibn al-Jawzī, *Nawāsikh* 315; Ibn Ḥazm 36).

22 Q 5.105

O believers, ***look after your own souls. He who is astray cannot hurt you, if you are rightly guided****. Unto God shall you return, all together, and He will tell you what you were doing.*

Commentary: The verse directs Muslims to take care of their own souls and good deeds and disregard or ignore the wrongful actions of nonbelievers. However, this principle of tolerance is abrogated by the Sword verse (Ibn al-Jawzī, *Nawāsikh*, 315).

23 Q 6.66

Thy people have cried it lies; yet it is the truth. ***Say: 'I am not a guardian over you.***

Commentary: Muḥammad declares in this verse that his mission is to only warn and give Islam's message, but this peaceful limited role has been abrogated by the Sword verse (Ibn Salāma 44; al-Naḥḥās 2: 318; Ibn al-Jawzī, *Nawāsikh* 324; al-Makkī 281).

24 Q 6.68

When thou seest those who plunge into Our signs, turn away from them *until they plunge into some other talk*;

Commentary: This verse requires Muḥammad to turn away from those who would deny Islam's message, but this requirement has been abrogated by the Sword verse (Ibn al-Jawzī, *Nawāsikh* 324; Shu'la 137).

25 Q 6.70

Leave alone those who take their religion for a sport and a diversion, *and whom the present life has deluded. Remind hereby, lest a soul should be given up to destruction for what it has earned; apart from God, it has no protector and no intercessor; though it offer any equivalent, it shall not be taken from it. Those are they who are given up to destruction for what they have earned; for them awaits a draught of boiling water and a painful chastisement, for that they were unbelievers.*

Commentary: The verse counsels Muslims to abandon polytheists to their worldly ways, because they (polytheists) will suffer severe consequences for their behavior. But this passive treatment of polytheists has been abrograted by the Sword verse (al-Naḥḥās 2: 321; al-Makkī 282; Ibn al-Jawzī, *Nawāsikh* 326).

26 Q 6.91

They measured not God with His true measure when they said, 'God has not sent down aught on any mortal.' Say: 'Who sent down the Book that Moses brought as a light and a guidance to men? You put it into parchments, revealing them, and hiding much; and you were taught that you knew not, you and your fathers.' ***Say: 'God.' Then leave them alone, playing their game of plunging.***

Commentary: In the verse the directive of staying away from nonbelievers (in this case, Jews or polytheists) and their misbelief is abrogated by the Sword verse (Ibn Salāma 45; Ibn al-Jawzī, *Nawāsikh* 327; Ibn Ḥazm 37).

27 Q 6.104

Clear proofs have come to you from your Lord. ***Whoso sees clearly, it is to his own gain, and whoso is blind, it is to his own loss; I am not a watcher over you.***

Commentary: The verse declares that faith in Islam is left to individual choice (and not Muḥammad's authority), but this declaration is abrogated by the Sword verse (Ibn Salāma 45; Ibn al-Jawzī, *Nawāsikh* 327; Ibn Ḥazm 37).

28 Q 6.106

Follow thou what has been revealed to thee from thy Lord; there is no god but He; ***and turn thou away from the idolaters.***

Commentary: Muḥammad is commanded in this text to avoid the polytheists and their words. This command is abrogated later by the Sword verse (Ibn Salāma 45; Ibn al-Jawzī, *Nawāsikh* 328; al-Makkī 286; Ibn Ḥazm 37).

29 Q 6.107

Had God willed, they were not idolaters; ***and We have not appointed thee a watcher over them, neither art thou their guardian.***

Commentary: This verse addresses Muḥammad, stating that his mission is to fulfill Allah's message; he has no authority over the polytheists and their beliefs. However, the Sword verse has abrogated this message that Muḥammad has no authority over the polytheists (Ibn Salāma 45; Ibn al-Jawzī, *Nawāsikh* 328; Ibn Ḥazm 38).

NOTE: With this abrogation Muḥammad and, later by extension, all Muslims, become in charge of all creation: to compel anyone to Islam and force others to pay the tribute (*jizya*).

30 Q 6.108

Abuse not those to whom they pray, apart from God, or they will abuse God in revenge without knowledge. *So We have decked out fair to every nation their deeds; then to their Lord they shall return, and He will tell them what they have been doing.*

Commentary: To prevent the cursing of Allah by polytheists, this verse forbids Muslims from cursing the Quraysh gods. However, some scholars state that this prohibition has been abrogated by the Sword verse, because its command to kill infidels is a stronger action than merely cursing nonbelievers or their gods. With the abrogation of this verse, there is thus no reason to stop cursing the gods of others (Ibn Salāma 45-46; Ibn al-Jawzī, *Nawāsikh* 329; Ibn Ḥazm 38).

NOTE: Consequently, the laws in Islamic countries criminalize those who would criticize Islam and permit Muslims to insult followers of other religions.

31 Q 6.112

So We have appointed to every Prophet an enemy—Satans of men and jinn, revealing tawdry speech to each other, all as a delusion; yet, had thy Lord willed, they would never have done it. ***So leave them to their forging,***

Commentary: Scholars state that the allowance and tolerance of misbelievers as advocated in this verse is abrogated by the Sword verse (Ibn Salāma 46; Ibn al-Jawzī, *Nawāsikh* 329; Ibn Ḥazm 38).

32 Q 6.135

Say (O Muḥammad...): "O my people! Work according to your way, surely, I too am working (in my way), and you will come to know for which of us will be the (happy) end in the Hereafter. Certainly the *Zâlimûn* (polytheists and wrongdoers, etc.) will not be successful." (Hilâlî-Khân trans.)

Commentary: Scholars who interpret this verse to mean no compulsion to convert nonbelievers to Islam, state that this verse is abrogated by the Sword verse (Ibn Salāma 46; Ibn al-Jawzī, *Nawāsikh* 330; Ibn Ḥazm 38).

33 Q 6.158

What, do they look for the angels to come to them, nothing less, or that thy Lord should come, or that one of thy Lord's signs should come? On the day that one of thy Lord's signs comes it shall not profit a soul to believe that never believed before, or earned some good in his belief. ***Say: 'Watch and wait; We too are waiting.'***

Commentary: Even though disbelievers of Muḥammad's call will lose their souls on the Day of Judgment by waiting for a miraculous sign from Allah during their earthly life, the verse counsels Muḥammad to respond to them that he is waiting too; there is nothing else he needs to do, as the disbelievers will be condemned at their death. However, this passive waiting to witness the disbelievers' doom at their death has been abrogated by the Sword verse (Ibn Salāma 46; Ibn al-Jawzī, *Nawāsikh* 337).

34 Q 6.159

Those who have made divisions in their religion and become sects, ***thou art not of them in anything;*** *their affair is unto God, then He will tell them what they have been doing.*

Commentary: The verse calls upon Muslims to disassociate themselves with non-Muslims (Jews, Christians, and other religious groups; see Ibn Kathīr 6: 240 and al-Tabarī 10: 34) and their subgroups as Allah will decide their fate. However, this call is abrogated by the Sword verse (Ibn al-Jawzī, *Nawāsikh* 337; Shu'la 140; Ibn Ḥazm 38).

35 Q 7.180

To God belong the Names Most Beautiful; so call Him by them, and leave those who blaspheme His Names*—they shall assuredly be recompensed for the things they did.*

Commentary: Though this verse commands Muslims to leave idolaters alone, most the Islamic scholars state that this verse's command is abrogated by the Sword verse (Ibn al-Jawzī, *Nawāsikh* 339; Ibn Ḥazm 38).

36 Q 7.183

and I respite them—assuredly My guile is sure.

Commentary: Some Islamic scholars interpret the phrase *"I respite them"* to mean that Muḥammad does not need to involve himself with polytheists; Allah will deal with them and their sins. However, the Sword verse abrogates this verse and its prerogative by commanding all Muslims to deal with these nonbelievers for their sins (Ibn Salāma 47).

37a Q 7.199

Take the abundance*, and bid to what is honourable,...*

Commentary: Some scholars state that the verse expresses leniency toward polytheists, but this provision has been abrogated by the Sword verse (Ibn al-Jawzī, *Nawāsikh* 341; al-Makkī 292; Shu'la 141).

37b Q 7.199
*...**and turn away from the ignorant.***

Commentary: The term *"the ignorant"* refers to the polytheists and means that the verse commands Muslims to avoid the polytheists. But this verse's command has been abrogated by the Sword verse (Ibn Salāma 47; Ibn al-Jawzī, *Nawāsikh* 341; al-Makkī 293; Ibn Ḥazm 38).

38 Q 8.61
And if they incline to peace, do thou incline to it; and put thy trust in God; He is the All-hearing, the All-knowing.

Commentary: According to some interpretations, the verse is discussing polytheists, stating that Muslims can maintain a peaceful relationship with them if the polytheists are peaceful toward the Muslims. However, peace agreements with polytheists (and eventually all non-Muslims) are abrogated by the Sword verse (Ibn al-Jawzī, *Nawāsikh* 347-348; al-Makkī 300).

39 Q 9.7
*How should the idolaters have a covenant with God and His Messenger? **—excepting those with whom you made covenant at the Holy Mosque; so long as they go straight with you, do you go straight with them;** surely God loves the godfearing.*

Commentary: The exegetes differ about the identity of the treaty partner mentioned in this verse: Banū Damra, Quraysh, or Khuzā'a. (For instance, at the Treaty of Hudaybīya, the Muslims, already allied with the Khuzā'a, brokered a truce with their enemy, the Quraysh (Ibn al-Jawzī, *Nawāsikh* 361-362). This treaty has been abrogated by the Sword verse (Ibn Salāma 51; Ibn al-Jawzī, *Nawāsikh* 362).

40 Q 10.20

They say, 'Why has a sign not been sent down upon him from his Lord?' Say: 'The Unseen belongs only to God. ***Then watch and wait; I shall be with you watching and waiting.****'*

Commentary: The verse declares that Muḥammad, like the polytheists, must wait for Allah to show miracles to them. Also, this verse contains no threat against the polytheists. However, this waiting for Allah to show miracles has been abrogated by the Sword verse (Ibn Salāma 53; Ibn Ḥazm 41).

NOTE: When the Sword verse came to Muḥammad, it abrogated the need for signs (miracles) to prove the prophethood of Muḥammad, as the "sword" then became the proof.

41 Q 10.41

If they cry lies to thee, then do thou say: 'I have my work, and you have your work; *you are quit of what I do, and I am quit of what you do.'*

Commentary : The verse directs Muḥammad to answer the accusations of the polytheists with, *"I have my work,"* meaning each group—Muslims and polytheists—are responsible only for themselves. However, this tolerance for non-Muslims is abrogated by the Sword verse (Ibn Salāma 54; Ibn al-Jawzī, *Nawāsikh* 372; Ibn Ḥazm 41).

NOTE: Muḥammad upheld this peaceful policy (as shown in this verse) while he and his followers lived in Mecca, weak and few in number. Once Muḥammad gained military strength and thousands of followers in Medina, the policy outlined in Q 10.41 was abrogated by the Sword verse.

42 Q 10.46

Whether We show thee a part of that We promise them, or We call thee unto Us, to Us they shall return; then God is witness of the things they do.

Commentary: The verse informs Muḥammad that he might see glimpses of the defeat and suffering that the polytheists will face or he might die before that sight; but in all cases their fate is in the hands of Allah, who will punish them for their acts. However, the principle of leaving the judgment of polytheists only to God is abrogated by the Sword verse (Ibn Salāma 54).

43 Q 10.99

And if thy Lord had willed, whoever is in the earth would have believed, all of them, all together. ***Wouldst thou then constrain the people, until they are believers?***

Commentary: This verse states that Allah can make all people believers of Muḥammad's message, but Muḥammad cannot force people to embrace Islam. However, the restraint (except for Allah) against forced conversion to Islam mentioned in this verse is abrogated by the Sword verse (Ibn Salāma 54; Shu'la 146).

44 Q 10.102

Then do they wait for (anything) save for (destruction) like the days of the men who passed away before them? Say: "**Wait then, I am (too) with you among those who wait.**" (Hilâlî-Khân trans.)

Commentary: The verse contains a threat to the Meccan polytheists: a torment will come upon them soon, similar to the devastating punishments suffered by rebellious nations before them. And according to the verse, Muḥammad himself will wait for this calamitous day. But this waiting for Allah's punishment has been abrogated by the Sword verse (Ibn Salāma 54; Ibn Ḥazm 41).

NOTE: Though this verse initially concerned the Meccan pagans, it later became an established rule toward all people of other faiths. However, with its abrogation by the Sword verse, Muḥammad no longer needed to wait for Allah's wrath upon anyone (polytheists or other non-Muslims) who rejected Muḥammad's Da'wa, or call; he himself now had the authority to judge and bring torment upon them for their misbelief.

45 Q 10.108

Say: 'O men, the truth has come to you from your Lord. ***Whosoever is guided is guided only to his own gain, and whosoever goes astray, it is only to his own loss. I am not a guardian over you.****'*

Commentary: This verse directs Muḥammad to tell others that whoever is guided to Islam and believes, does so for the good of his soul, and whoever goes astray, rejecting the call of Muḥammad, does so to his own detriment; Muḥammad is not part of this personal decision. However, according to a team of scholars, this statement allowing for self-determination in choosing Islam has been completely abrogated by the Sword verse (Ibn Salāma 54; Ibn Ḥazm 41).

NOTE: After the Sword verse came, the new rule became these two enforced choices: acceptance of Islam or death. People of the Book (Jews and Christians) could avoid death by paying a head tax (*jizya*).

46 Q 10.109

And follow thou what is revealed to thee; ***and be thou patient until God shall judge;*** *and He is the best of judges.*

Commentary: The verse counsels Muḥammad to remain patient and let Allah judge Muḥammad's rejecters. However, this policy of patience regarding Muḥammad's opponents is abrogated by the Sword verse (Ibn Salāma 54; Shu'la 146).

NOTE: This verse illustrates Muḥammad's policy of patience with his critics during his time in Mecca. Once Muḥammad migrated to Medina and developed a formidable military force there, the Sword verse was "revealed" to him. The Sword verse was then used to abrogate this Meccan policy and apply its own new rules.

47 Q 11.12

Perchance thou art leaving part of what is revealed to thee, and thy breast is straitened by it, because they say, 'Why has a treasure not been sent down upon him, or an angel not come with him?' ***Thou art only a warner; and God is a Guardian over everything.***

Commentary: Though this verse relegates Muḥammad's role to simply a warner to his people, Muslim scholars state that this limitation has been abrogated by the Sword verse (Ibn Salāma 55; Ibn al-Jawzī, *Nawāsikh* 375).

48 Q 11.121

And say to the unbelievers: 'Act you according to your station; we are acting.

Commentary: The verse's message, addressed to Muḥammad, calls for tolerance and not harassment of nonbelievers. But this restraint is abrogated by the Sword verse (Ibn Salāma 55; Ibn al-Jawzī, *Nawāsikh* 376; Ibn Ḥazm 41).

49 Q 11.122

And watch and wait; we are also watching and waiting.'

Commentary: Similar to the preceding verse, this one also calls for Muḥammad to tolerate nonbelievers and their actions. This rule too is abrogated by the Sword verse (Ibn Salāma 55; Ibn al-Jawzī, *Nawāsikh* 376; Ibn Ḥazm 41).

50 Q 13.40

Whether We show thee a part of that We promise them, or We call thee to Us, it is thine only to deliver the Message, and Ours the reckoning.

Commentary: This verse requires Muḥammad only to convey Allah's message and leave the judgment of nonbelievers (including polytheists and People of the Book) to Allah, but this charge is abrogated by the Sword verse (Ibn Salāma 57; Ibn al-Jawzī, *Nawāsikh* 378; Ibn Ḥazm 42).

51 Q 15.3

leave them to eat, and to take their joy, and to be bemused by hope; certainly they will soon know!

Commentary: The verse commands Muḥammad to let the polytheists enjoy their worldly pleasures and false hopes without interference, because they will eventually learn their true miserable fate. This prescribed acquiescence is abrogated by the Sword verse (Ibn Salāma 58; Ibn al-Jawzī, *Nawāsikh* 379; Ibn Ḥazm 42).

52 Q 15.85

We created not the heavens and the earth, and all that is between them, save in truth. Surely the Hour is coming; ***so pardon thou, with a gracious pardoning.***

Commentary: The verse reminds Muḥammad that the time of judgment is coming and that he must treat polytheists with kindly forgiveness. But this verse's request for Muḥammad to forgive nonbelievers is abrogated by the Sword verse (Ibn Salāma 58; Ibn Ḥazm 42-43; Shu'la 149).

53a Q 15.88

Look not with your eyes ambitiously at what We have bestowed on certain classes of them (the disbelievers),... (Hilâlî-Khân trans.)

Commentary: The verse admonishes Muḥammad (and later on, all Muslims) not to covet the good things that Allah has given to some polytheists. However, this directive against jealousy of polytheists and their property has been abrogated by the Sword verse (Ibn Sālama 58).

NOTE: This abrogation by the Sword verse means that Muslims can act on these feelings of envy with impunity.

53b Q 15.88

...nor grieve over them. And lower your wings for the believers (be courteous to the fellow-believers). (Hilâlî-Khân trans.)

Commentary: Some commentators state that Muḥammad is told in this verse to not worry about or feel sorry for the polytheists who reject Islam. According to these same commentators, this verse is abrogated by the Sword verse (Ibn al-Jawzī, *Nawāsikh* 381; Ibn Ḥazm 43).

NOTE: With the Sword verse, Muḥammad can punish the polytheists for their rejection of his message without any worry or sorrow.

54 Q 15.89

and say, 'Surely, I am the manifest warner.'

Commentary: The declaration in the verse that Muḥammad is only a plain warner has been abrogated by the Sword verse (Ibn Salāma 58; Ibn Ḥazm 43).

NOTE: This verse suggests that punishment of nonbelievers will be divinely administered. However, the abrogation of Q 15.89 by the Sword verse indicates that this punishment can also be humanly administered.

55 Q 15.94

So shout that thou art commanded and turn thou away from the idolaters.

Commentary: This verse, addressed to Muḥammad, tells him to disregard the polytheists if they reject Allah and worship others, but this directive is abrogated by the Sword verse (Ibn Salāma 58; al-Naḥḥās 2: 482; Ibn al-Jawzī, *Nawāsikh* 382).

56 Q 16.82

So, if they turn their backs, thine it is only to deliver the manifest Message.

Commentary: This verse tells Muḥammad that if the polytheists ignore him his only duty is to preach his message. But this limited authority is abrogated by the Sword verse (Ibn Salāma 59; Ibn al-Jawzī, *Nawāsikh* 386).

57 Q 16.106

Whoever disbelieved in Allah after his belief, except him who is forced thereto and whose heart is at rest with Faith but such as open their breasts to disbelief, on them is wrath from Allah, and theirs will be a great torment. (Hilâlî-Khân trans.)

Commentary: According to this verse, a believer who recants his faith publicly under pressure but still inwardly believes will not be punished. However, some scholars state that this exemption is abrogated by the Sword verse, unless the person is practicing *taqīya*, an Islamic principle where Muslims may denounce or conceal their faith to protect themselves from imminent harm or protect or further the interests of Islam (Ibn Salāma 59; Ibn Ḥazm 43).

58 Q 16.125

Call thou to the way of thy Lord with wisdom and good admonition, and dispute with them in the better way. *Surely thy Lord knows very well those who have gone astray from His way, and He knows very well those who are guided.*

Commentary: This verse urges Muḥammad to use wisdom and kindness when preaching to and reasoning with the polytheists (a policy followed by Muḥammad in Mecca). But a team of scholars state that this approach in this verse is abrogated by the Sword verse (Ibn Salāma 60; al-Naḥḥās 2: 487; Ibn al-Jawzī, *Nawāṣikh* 387; Ibn Ḥazm 43-44; al-Makkī 336).

59 Q 16.126

And if you punish (your enemy, O you believers in the Oneness of Allah), then punish them with the like of that with which you were afflicted! But if you endure patiently, verily, it is better for the patient. (Hilâlî-Khân trans.)

Commentary: The verse commands Muslims to fight those who declare war on them, using the same means as their enemies, but patience is the best recourse. However, the Sword verse abrogates this condition of retaliation or peaceful patience (Ibn al-Jawzī, *Nawāsikh* 388).

NOTE: The Sword verse now commands Muslims to fight non-Muslims any time and any place, even if non-Muslims did not initiate the war.

60 Q 16.127

And be patient; *yet is thy patience only with the help of God. And do not sorrow for them, nor be thou straitened for what they devise.*

Commentary: In this verse, Muslims are encouraged to practice patience—with the help of Allah—when dealing with the polytheists and not be troubled by the unbelievers' plans. Some scholars state that this appeal to patience is abrogated by the Sword verse (Ibn Salāma 60; Ibn al-Jawzī, *Nawāsikh* 389; Ibn Ḥazm 44; Shu'la 151).

61 Q 17.54

Your Lord knows you very well; if He will, He will have mercy on you, or, if He will, He will chastise you. ***We sent thee not to be a guardian over them****.*

Commentary: The verse explains that Muḥammad was not sent from Allah to take charge of or advocate for people (but to deliver only Allah's message). However, some scholars state that this limitation in Muḥammad's role has been abrogated by the Sword verse (Ibn Salāma 61; Ibn Ḥazm 44).

62 Q 19.39

Warn thou them of the day of anguish*, when the matter shall be determined, and they yet heedless and unbelieving.*

Commentary: In this verse, Muḥammad is required to warn the polytheists of the consequences of not believing in Islam and the Day of Judgment. But some scholars state that this call for "warnings only" is abrogated by the Sword verse, which requires fighting those who refuse to accept Islam (Ibn Salāma 62; Ibn Ḥazm 44).

63 Q 19.75

Say: 'Whosoever is in error, let the All-merciful prolong his term for him! *Till, when they see that they were threatened, whether the chastisement, or the Hour, then they shall surely know who is worse in place, and who is weaker in hosts.'*

Commentary: Addressing Muḥammad, this verse tells him to respond to the polytheists (who think they are better and stronger than Muḥammad and his followers) that Allah will give the polytheists respite until they see their promised punishment (on earth or at the Day of Judgment)—at which time, they will then know who is better and stronger (Muslims). However, waiting for Allah to deliver this punishment on earth is abrogated by the Sword verse (Ibn Salāma 62; Ibn Ḥazm 44).

64 Q 19.84

So ***hasten thou not against them;*** *We are only numbering for them a number.*

Commentary: The verse requires Muḥammad not to pray for Allah's punishment on his rejecters but let them incriminate themselves to Allah for their sins; Allah will judge them. However, this directive has been abrogated by the Sword verse (Ibn Salāma 62; Ibn Ḥazm 45).

NOTE: When Muḥammad immigrated to Medina he himself tormented non-Muslims, contrary to his peaceful actions in Mecca.

65 Q 20.130

So be thou patient under what they say*, and proclaim thy Lord's praise before the rising of the sun, and before its setting, and proclaim thy Lord's praise in the watches of the night, and at the ends of the day; haply thou wilt be well-pleasing.*

Commentary: The verse tells Muḥammad to show restraint in the face of his critics (who denounce him as a madman or a magician) and respond instead with praise and glorification of Allah. However, this forbearance toward his critics is abrogated by the Sword verse (Ibn Salāma 64; Ibn al-Jawzī, *Nawāsikh* 399; Ibn Ḥazm 45; Shu'la 154).

66 Q 20.135
***Say: 'Everyone is waiting; so wait**, and assuredly you shall know who are the travellers on the even path, and who is guided.'*

Commentary: The verse counsels Muḥammad to tell his followers to wait for Allah's signs like everyone else because when the end comes they (polytheists) will know who follows the right way of Allah. However, this directive to bide one's time and let Allah reveal the true believers has been abrogated by the Sword verse (Ibn Salāma 64; Ibn al-Jawzī, *Nawāsikh* 399; Ibn Ḥazm 44; Shu'la 154).

67 Q 22.49
Say: 'O men, I am only for you a plain warner.'

Commentary: In this verse, Muḥammad clearly defines his mission here: he is just a warner and not an enforcer. However, this limited authority is abrogated by the Sword verse (Ibn Salāma 66).

68 Q 22.68
And if they should dispute with thee, do thou say, 'God knows very well what you are doing.

Commentary: In this verse, Muḥammad is commanded to give to those who wish to argue with him this reply, which leaves the final word to Allah. This deflection has been abrogated by the Sword verse (Ibn Salāma 66; Ibn al-Jawzī, *Nawāsikh* 400; Shu'la 155).

NOTE: With this abrogation, Muḥammad no longer had to avoid controversy and could apply the Sword verse in such cases.

69 Q 23.54
So leave thou them in their perplexity for a time.

Commentary: After discussing the folly and errors of believers of other faiths in the preceding verses, this verse states that Muslims should leave nonbelievers to their own religious ignorance. However, this religious tolerance is abrogated by the Sword verse (Ibn Salāma 67; Ibn al-Jawzī, *Nawāsikh* 402; Ibn Ḥazm 46).

70 Q 23.96

Repel thou the evil with that which is fairer. *We Ourselves know very well that they describe.*

Commentary: The verse addresses Muḥammad, commanding him to counter the evil actions of his enemies with goodness, tolerance, and patience. However, this passive, tolerant response to his enemies has been abrogated by the Sword verse (Ibn Salāma 67; Ibn Ḥazm 46; Shu'la 156).

NOTE: With the abrogation of this verse by Q 9.5, Muḥammad no longer needs to use forgiveness and patience to fight his enemies but can apply instead a more combative, violent approach.

71 Q 24.54

Say: 'Obey God, and obey the Messenger; ***then, if you turn away, only upon him rests what is laid on him, and upon you rests what is laid on you.*** *If you obey him, you will be guided.* ***It is only for the Messenger to deliver the manifest Message.****'*

Commentary: The verse tells everyone to obey Allah and his messenger Muḥammad, but that Muḥammad's mission is only to convey the message of God. Those who choose to disregard Muḥammad's message will suffer the consequences, but Muḥammad will not be blamed because he is merely a guide or messenger. Muḥammad's limited role is abrogated by the Sword verse (Ibn Salāma 70; Ibn Ḥazm 48; Shu'la 157-158).

72 Q 25.43

Hast thou seen him who has taken his caprice to be his god? ***Wilt thou be a guardian over them?***

Commentary: The verse asks if Muḥammad can coerce those whose god is their ego to believe in Islam, implying that he cannot. Some Muslim scholars state that this lack of oversight is abrogated by the Sword verse (Ibn al-Jawzī, *Nawāsikh* 414; Shu'la 159).

73 Q 25.63

The servants of the All-merciful are those who walk in the earth modestly and who, ***when the ignorant address them, say, 'Peace'****;*

Commentary: The verse claims that the faithful servants of the Merciful (Allah) will respond to the speech of the nonbelievers with patient wisdom, but a team of scholars states that this benevolent response is abrogated by the Sword verse (Ibn Ḥazm 49).

74 Q 27.92

and to recite the Koran. So whosoever is guided, is only guided to his own gain; and whosoever goes astray, say: 'I am naught but a warner.

Commentary: In this verse Muḥammad declares that reciting the Qur'ān is sufficient, and each human being bears the consequences of his or her own response. Muḥammad only bears the responsibility of being the warner. Muḥammad's role as only a warner has been abrogated by the Sword verse (Ibn Salāma 72; Ibn al-Jawzī, *Nawāsikh* 419; Ibn Ḥazm 49; Shu'la 160).

75 Q 28.55

When they hear idle talk, they turn away from it and say, 'We have our deeds, and you your deeds. Peace be upon you! We desire not the ignorant.'

Commentary: The verse instructs believers to withdraw from those nonbelievers, who utter vain or idle talk, and say only to them, *"We have our deeds, and you have your deeds,"* ending the conversation with an affirmation of peace with the nonbelievers but not an acceptance of their ways. This principle is generally acknowledged as abrogated, with some scholars stating that it is abrogated by the Sword verse (Ibn Salāma 72; Ibn al-Jawzī, *Nawāsikh* 420-421; Ibn Ḥazm 49).

76 Q 29.50

They say, 'Why have signs not been sent down upon him from his Lord?' Say: 'The signs are only with God, ***and I am only a plain warner.'***

Commentary: The verse maintains that the mission of Muḥammad is simply to warn people. This limitation of Muḥammad's mission is abrogated by the Sword verse (Ibn Salāma 73).

77 Q 30.60

So be thou patient; surely God's promise is true; *and let not those who have not sure faith make thee unsteady.*

Commentary: This verse, which addresses Muḥammad, advises him to maintain his patience with those Quraysh tribesmen who have disdained his call and not let their rejection shake his faith. Some scholars state that this verse is Meccan in revelation, and therefore the command for patience is abrogated by the Medinan Sword verse (Ibn Salāma 74; Ibn al-Jawzī, *Nawāsikh* 425).

78 Q 31.23

And whoso disbelieves, let not his disbelief grieve thee; unto Us they shall return, *and We shall tell them what they did. Surely God knows all the thoughts within the breasts.*

Commentary: This verse, addressed to Muḥammad, tells him not to grieve because his people don't believe in him, because Allah will judge the rejecters on the Day of Resurrection. Some commentators state that disregard for misbelief is abrogated by the Sword verse (Ibn al-Jawzī, *Nawāsikh* 426).

79 Q 32.30

So turn thou away from them, and wait; they too are waiting.

Commentary: The verse directs Muḥammad to turn from the polytheists and other nonbelievers and wait to see what Allah will do, but this directive to wait has been abrogated by the Sword verse. Commenting on this verse, Ibn al-Jawzī states that any text in the Qur'ān containing the phrase "turn from them" and the word "wait" has been abrogated (Ibn Salāma 74; Ibn al-Jawzī, *Nawāsikh* 427).

80 Q 33.48

And obey not the unbelievers and the hypocrites; heed not their hurt, *but put thy trust in God; God suffices as a guardian.*

Commentary: The verse requests from Muḥammad two actions: (1) trust Allah and not obey the unbelievers and hypocrites and (2) cause no harm to them. The second action is abrogated by the Sword verse (Ibn Salāma 74; Ibn al-Jawzī, *Nawāsikh* 428; Ibn Ḥazm 51).

81 Q 34.25

Say: 'You will not be questioned concerning our sins, neither shall we be questioned as to what you do.'

Commentary: This verse addresses Muḥammad, requesting him to tell polytheists that on the Day of Resurrection each will be responsible and judged according to his or her own behavior, but this postponement of judgment for polytheists to the Day of Resurrection is abrogated by the Sword verse (Ibn Salāma 75; Ibn al-Jawzī, *Nawāsikh* 434; Ibn Ḥazm 51).

82 Q 35.23

thou art naught but a warner.

Commentary: The verse describes Muḥammad as only a warner, but this limited role is abrogated by the Sword verse (Ibn Salāma 75; Ibn al-Jawzī, *Nawāsikh* 435).

83 Q 36.76

So do not let their saying grieve thee*; assuredly We know what they keep secret and what they publish.*

Commentary: The verse, addressed to Muḥammad, comforts him, explaining that Allah knows both the secret and public criticism of Muḥammad by his detractors. The verse also hints of eventual punishment (in the hereafter) for these critics. Some scholars state that grief and pardon for polytheists is abrogated by the Sword verse (Ibn Salāma 75).

84 Q 37.174
So turn thou from them for a while,

Commentary: The verse commands Muḥammad to disregard the disbelievers *"for a while."* The abrogation here of this verse is related to the commentators' understanding of the phrase *"for a while"*:
(1) time when the fighting command is revealed
(2) time when the disbelievers are dead and must give an account of their earthly works on the Day of Judgment
(3) Day of Resurrection
Those commentators who agree that the verse is abrogated choose interpretations (2) and (3) and state that this policy of avoiding the disbelievers is abrogated by the Sword verse. (Ibn Salāma 76; Ibn Ḥazm 52).

85 Q 37.175
and see them; soon they shall see!

Commentary: The verse tells Muḥammad that if he watches the polytheists, he will eventually see them punished. According to al-Tabarī, the polytheists "will see what will come upon them from our [Allah's] punishment, when repentance will no longer benefit them, when the affliction of Allah comes down on them." This punishment by Allah alone is abrogated by the Sword verse (Ibn Salāma 76; Ibn al-Jawzī, *Nawāsikh* 437; Ibn Ḥazm 52).

86 Q 37.178
So turn thou from them for a while,

Commentary: The verse commands Muḥammad to disregard his enemies for a period of time, but this command to avoid them is abrogated by the Sword verse (Ibn Salāma 76). (For discussion about *"a while,"* see the commentary for Q 37.174.)

NOTE: This verse implies that these nonbelievers will be reckoned with later. Whether this reckoning is a worldly or otherworldly threat is not clear. However, this issue becomes moot with the abrogation of Q 37.178 by the Sword verse.

87 Q 38.70

This alone is revealed to me, that I am only a clear warner.'

Commentary: This verse declares (again) that Muḥammad is just a simple warner, but this limited role is abrogated by the Sword verse (Ibn Salāma 76).

88 Q 39.3

*Belongs not sincere religion to God? And those who take protectors, apart from Him—'We only serve them that they may bring us nigh in nearness to God'—**surely God shall judge between them touching that whereon they are at variance**. Surely God guides not him who is a liar, unthankful.*

Commentary: The verse states that those who believe in additional gods as well as Allah for protective measures will be judged by Allah for not worshipping only Allah. However, leaving the decision to condemn the polytheists only to Allah on the Day of Judgment has been abrogated by the Sword Verse (Ibn Salāma 77; Ibn al-Jawzī, *Nawāsikh* 441; Ibn Ḥazm 52).

NOTE: According to al-Tabarī (20: 157), this verse includes Jews and Christians in this judgment and thus expands the number of the condemned. (See the section Qur'ānic Definition of "Idolaters," page 44.) This interpretation and the verse's abrogation by the Sword verse means Muslims can not only judge people of other faiths, they have been ordered to kill them.

89 Q 39.15

***so serve what you will apart from Him**.' Say: 'Surely the losers are they who lose themselves and their families on the Day of Resurrection; is not that the manifest loss?*

Commentary: This verse is addressing Muḥammad, telling him to follow a policy of "religious laissez-faire" with nonbelievers, where he would abstain from trying to change or interfere with their beliefs but know they and their families would lose their souls on the Day of Judgment. However, this policy of noninterference with the worship of nonbelievers has been abrogated by the Sword verse (Ibn Salāma 77; Ibn Ḥazm 52).

90 Q 39.39
Say, o my people, do ye act according to your state; verily I will act [according to mine]: hereafter shall ye know (Sale trans.)

Commentary: In this verse, Muḥammad is directed to tell the polytheists that they do whatever they can and he will do likewise, and, in the hereafter, they will know what was right. Some scholars state that postponement of judgment to the hereafter is abrogated by the Sword verse (Ibn Salāma 77; Ibn Ḥazm 53).

91 Q 39.40
on which of us will be inflicted a punishment that shall cover him with shame, and on whom a lasting punishment shall fall. (Sale trans.)

Commentary: This verse contains a warning—that the opponents of Muḥammad will be disgraced in the hereafter, followed by eternal punishment. But this postponement of eternal punishment to the hereafter is abrogated by the Sword verse (Ibn Salāma 77; Ibn Ḥazm 53).

92 Q 39.41
Surely We have sent down upon thee the Book for mankind with the truth. ***Whosoever is guided, is only guided to his own gain, and whosoever goes astray, it is only to his own loss; thou art not a guardian over them.***

Commentary: The verse states that the Qur'ān was revealed for all people, who are free to accept (or not) its guidance for their benefit or detriment; they, and not Muḥammad, are accountable for their own actions. A group of Muslim scholars, however, state that this personal freedom to choose has been abrogated by the Sword verse (Ibn Salāma 78; Ibn Ḥazm 53).

93 Q 39.46

Say: 'O God, Thou originator of the heavens and the earth who knowest the Unseen and the Visible, Thou shalt judge between Thy servants touching that whereon they are at variance.'

Commentary: This verse affirms that Muḥammad should ask Allah, the creator of the heavens and earth, to judge disagreements between Muḥammad and his people. This deference to Allah as the sole judge over men has been abrogated by the Sword verse (Ibn Salāma 78; Ibn Ḥazm 53).

94 Q 40.12

That is because, when God was called to alone, you disbelieved; but if others are associated with Him, then you believe. ***Judgment belongs to God, the All-high, the All-great.***

Commentary: This verse declares that judgment belongs solely to Allah, but Allah's singular authority to judge is abrogated by the Sword verse (Ibn Salāma 78).

95 Q 40.55

So be thou patient; surely God's promise is true*....*

Commentary: This verse requests Muḥammad to be patient, but this appeal to Muḥammad to remain patient is abrogated by the Sword verse (Ibn Ḥazm 53).

96 Q 40.77

So be thou patient; surely God's promise is true*....*

Commentary: See the commentary for Q 40.55 (Ibn Ḥazm 53).

97 Q 41.34

Not equal are the good deed and the evil deed. Repel with that which is fairer *and behold, he between whom and thee there is enmity shall be as if he were a loyal friend.*

Commentary: Muḥammad is advised to face evil deeds by others by responding with a better action, so that his enemies might become friends. However, this call to subdue evil with positive behavior has been abrogated by the Sword verse (Ibn Salāma 79; Ibn al-Jawzī, *Nawāsikh* 445; Ibn Ḥazm 53).

NOTE: Even without the Islamic doctrine of abrogation, the Qur'ān contains few moral principles promoting virtuous behavior in social situations (e.g., ignoring the mockery of critics, answering the rejection of disbelievers with kindness, etc.).

98 Q 42.6

And those who have taken to them protectors apart from Him—God is Warden over them; ***thou art not a guardian over them.***

Commentary: This verse states that Allah, and not Muḥammad, is the guardian of the polytheists, but Muḥammad's restricted authority here has been abrogated by the Sword verse (Ibn Salāma 79; Ibn Ḥazm 54).

99 Q 42.15

Therefore call thou, and go straight as thou hast been commanded; do not follow their caprices. And say: 'I believe in whatever Book God has sent down; I have been commanded to be just between you. God is our Lord and your Lord. ***We have our deeds, and you have your deeds; there is no argument between us and you; God shall bring us together, and unto Him is the homecoming.****'*

Commentary: In this verse, Muḥammad declares to Jews and Christians that Allah is his and their God, even as Muslims and they differ in their deeds. Still, there is no enmity over these differences because God will gather all of them together (al-Tabarī 20: 487). But, the Sword verse abrogates this verse's declaration for peaceful acceptance of these differences (Ibn Salāma 79; Ibn al-Jawzī, *Nawāsikh* 449).

NOTE: This declaration supporting religious tolerance was revealed before the command to fight non-Muslims.

100 Q 42.48

If then they run away, We have not sent thee as a guard over them. Thy duty is but to convey (the Message). And truly, when We give man a taste of a Mercy from Ourselves, he doth exult thereat, but when some ill happens to him, on account of the deeds which his hands have sent forth, truly then is man ungrateful! (Yusuf Ali trans.)

Commentary

The verse narrowly defines Muḥammad's mission as messenger—and not protector—of the people. However, this limit to Muḥammad's authority is abrogated by the Sword verse (Ibn Salāma 80; Ibn al-Jawzī, *Nawāsikh* 454; Ibn Ḥazm 55).

101 Q 43.83

Then leave them alone to plunge and play, until they encounter that day of theirs which they are promised.

Commentary: Muḥammad is commanded to disregard the foolish and frivolous actions of his rejecters until the Day of Resurrection. However, this restraint is abrogated by the Sword verse (Ibn Salāma 81; Ibn Ḥazm 55).

102 Q 43.89
yet pardon them, and say, 'Peace!' Soon they will know.

Commentary: The verse requests Muḥammad to condone the polytheists and respond to them in peace, but this request for tolerance is abrogated by the Sword verse (Ibn Salāma 81; Ibn al-Jawzī, *Nawāsikh* 455-456; Ibn Ḥazm 55).

103 Q 44.59
So be on the watch; they too are on the watch.

Commentary: In this verse Muḥammad is requested to wait, like everyone else, to see who will be the "winner" in the hereafter, but this waiting until the hereafter has been abrogated by the Sword verse (Ibn Salāma 81; Ibn al-Jawzī, *Nawāsikh* 457; Ibn Ḥazm 55).

104 Q 45.14
Say unto those who believe, that they forgive those who do not look for the days of God*, that He may recompense a people for that they have been earning.*

Commentary: The verse urges Muslims to forgive those people who have harmed them, but this request to forgive persecutors is abrogated by the Sword verse (Ibn Salāma 82; Ibn al-Jawzī, *Nawāsikh* 458-459; al-Naḥḥās 2: 625).

105 Q 46.35
So be thou patient, as the Messengers possessed of constancy were also patient*. Seek not to hasten it for them—it shall be as if on the day they see that they are promised, they had not tarried but for an hour of a single day. A Message to be delivered! And shall any be destroyed but the people of the ungodly?*

Commentary: This verse exhorts Muḥammad to be patient with the disbelievers, just like the earlier strong-willed apostles. But this counsel for patience is abrogated by the Sword verse (Ibn Salāma 85; Ibn al-Jawzī, *Nawāsikh* 465; Ibn Ḥazm 56).

106 Q 47.4
When you meet the unbelievers, smite their necks, then, when you have made wide slaughter among them, tie fast the bonds; ***then set them free, either by grace or ransom, till the war lays down its loads.*** *So it shall be; and if God had willed, He would have avenged Himself upon them; but that He may try some of you by means of others. And those who are slain in the way of God, He will not send their works astray.*

Commentary: The second part of this verse (to liberate or ransom captives until the war ends) has been abrogated by the Sword verse (Ibn Salāma 85; Ibn al-Jawzī, *Nawāsikh* 466; Ibn Ḥazm 56; al-Naḥḥās 3: 5).

107 Q 50.39
So be thou patient under what they say, *and proclaim thy Lord's praise before the rising of the sun, and before its setting,*

Commentary: This verse commands Muḥammad to be patient with his critics (who may have been Jews or polytheists according to the commentators; see Zamarkhsharī 5: 605), but this directive is abrogated by the Sword verse (Ibn Salāma 86).

108 Q 50.45
We know very well what they say; ***thou art not a tyrant over them. Therefore remind by the Koran him who fears My threat.***

Commentary: The verse tells Muḥammad to only admonish polytheists with the Qur'ān and forgo force because he does not have the authority to pressure them to believe. However, the use of only verbal warnings with polytheists is abrogated by the Sword verse (Ibn Salāma 86; Ibn al-Jawzī, *Nawāsikh* 470; Ibn Ḥazm 57).

109 Q 51.54
So turn thou from them; thou wilt not be reproached.

Commentary: The verse urges Muḥammad to disregard or withdraw from the disbelievers, for he will not be faulted for their rejection. However, this permitted passivity is abrogated by the Sword verse (Ibn al-Jawzī, *Nawāsikh* 472).

110 Q 52.31
Say: 'Await! I shall be awaiting with you.'

Commentary: The previous verse (Q 52.30) suggests that the Quraysh dismiss Muḥammad as an insignificant poet whose demise will eventually happen if they just wait. Muḥammad's response to this perception, as indicated by Q 52.31, is to wait also—but for the natural death of his critics (al-Tabarī 21: 594). However, this command to wait for their natural deaths is abrogated by the Sword verse (Ibn Salāma 87).

NOTE: Though this verse was initially addressed to the Quraysh, its abrogated ruling (which means, not waiting for non-Muslims to receive their eternal punishment at their natural deaths) is now applied as a general principle to all non-Muslims.

111 Q 52.45
Then leave them, till they encounter their day wherein they shall be thunderstruck,

Commentary: The verse tells Muḥammad to disregard the rejecters of his call, as they will eventually face their terrifying fate. This directive to Muḥammad to leave the rejecters alone is abrogated by the Sword verse (Ibn Salāma 87; Ibn al-Jawzī, *Nawāsikh* 473-474).

112 Q 52.48
And be thou patient under the judgment of thy Lord; surely thou art before Our eyes. *And proclaim the praise of thy Lord when thou arisest,*

Commentary: This verse requests Muḥammad to wait patiently despite the rejection of his call by his people, as Allah will judge them. However, this request to wait for Allah's judgment is abrogated by the Sword verse (Ibn Salāma 87; Ibn Ḥazm 58).

113 Q 53.29

So turn thou from him who turns away from Our Remembrance*, and desires only the present life.*

Commentary: The verse commands Muḥammad to turn away from those who rebuff his message and Qur'ān, preferring instead a worldly life. This command to withdraw from these rejecters is abrogated by the Sword verse (Ibn Salāma 87; Ibn al-Jawzī, *Nawāsikh* 475; Ibn Ḥazm 58).

114 Q 54.6

So turn thou away from them*. Upon the day when the Caller shall call unto a horrible thing,*

Commentary: The verse tells Muḥammad to leave alone those disbelievers of his message because they will be severely dealt with when the caller (a certain angel) comes to all mankind (al-Qurṭubī 20: 78). Again, this directive to ignore or disregard disbelievers, postponing their punishment to the end times, is considered abrogated by the Sword verse (Ibn Salāma 88).

115 Q 60.8

God forbids you not, as regards those who have not fought you in religion's cause*, nor expelled you from your habitations, that you should be kindly to them, and act justly towards them; surely God loves the just.*

Commentary: This verse states that Allah does not forbid Muslims to deal positively and justly with those non-Muslims who did not war against them because of religion or forced them out of their homes. However, this principle of dealing kindly with pacifist non-Muslims is abrogated by the Sword verse (Ibn Salāma 91; Ibn al-Jawzī, *Nawāsikh* 485; al-Naḥḥās 3: 67).

116 Q 60.9

God only forbids you as to those who have fought you in religion's cause*, and expelled you from your habitations, and have supported in your expulsion, that you should take them for friends. And whosoever takes them for friends, those—they are the evildoers.*

Commentary: See the commentary for Q 60.8 (Ibn Salāma 91; Ibn al-Jawzī, *Nawāsikh* 485; al-Naḥḥās 3: 67).

117 Q 60.10

O believers, when believing women come to you as emigrants, test them. God knows very well their belief. Then, if you know them to be believers, return them not to the unbelievers. They are not permitted to the unbelievers, nor are the unbelievers permitted to them. Give the unbelievers what they have expended; and there is no fault in you to marry them when you have given them their wages. Do not hold fast to the ties of unbelieving women, and ask what you have expended, and let them ask what they have expended. That is God's judgment; He judges between you; and God is All-knowing, All-wise.

Commentary: If Meccan women fleeing to Medina are Muslims, then their marriages to non-Muslim men are considered invalid and these wives cannot return to them. Any Muslim man in Medina is free to marry one of these refugee women, provided that he compensates the former husband by paying the woman's dowry. However, this provision to compensate the non-Muslim husband is abrogated by the Sword verse. (Ibn Salāma 92; Ibn al-Jawzī, *Nawāsikh* 491).

118 Q 64.14

O believers, among your wives and children there is an enemy to you; so beware of them. ***But if you pardon, and overlook, and if you forgive, surely God is All-forgiving, All-compassionate****.*

Commentary: The verse urges Muslims to forgive and pardon their family members, even if these wives and children are their enemies, but this compassionate forbearance toward family foes is abrogated by the Sword verse (Ibn al-Jawzī, *Nawāsikh* 492).

119 Q 68.44

So leave Me with him who cries lies to this discourse! *We will draw them on little by little whence they know not;*

Commentary: The verse commands Muḥammad to leave the issue of dealing with those who reject Muḥammad's message to Allah. However, this noninterference by Muḥammad is abrogated by the Sword verse (Ibn Salāma 94; Ibn al-Jawzī, *Nawāsikh* 494; Ibn Ḥazm 61).

120 Q 68.48

So be thou patient under the judgment of thy Lord*, and be not as the Man of the Fish, when he called, choking inwardly.*

Commentary: The verse requests Muḥammad to wait patiently for Allah's judgment (and not rage against Allah like Jonah), but this mandate for patience is considered abrogated by the Sword verse (Ibn Salāma 94; Ibn al-Jawzī, *Nawāsikh* 494; Ibn Ḥazm 61).

121 Q 70.5

So be thou patient with a sweet patience*;*

Commentary: The verse commands Muḥammad to endure his critics with commendable patience, but this *"sweet patience"* is abrogated by the Sword verse (Ibn Salāma 95; Ibn al-Jawzī, *Nawāsikh* 495).

122 Q 70.42

Then leave them alone to plunge and play *until they encounter that day of theirs which they are promised,*

Commentary: This verse requests Muḥammad to leave alone the polytheists, for they will eventually encounter their promised day of reckoning (and torment). However, this request to leave the misbelievers alone is abrogated by the Sword verse (Ibn Salāma 95; Ibn al-Jawzī, *Nawāsikh* 495).

123 Q 73.10
And bear thou patiently what they say, and forsake them graciously.

Commentary: The verse not only urges Muḥammad to be patient with the disbelievers but also withdraw from them in a gracious manner. However, some exegetes consider this directive abrogated by the Sword verse (Ibn Salāma 96; Ibn al-Jawzī, *Nawāsikh* 499; Ibn Ḥazm 62).

124 Q 74.11
Leave Me with him whom I created alone,

Commentary: In this verse, Allah is addressing Muḥammad, commanding Muḥammad to leave the rejecters, whom God created, to himself, but this command is considered abrogated by the Sword verse (Ibn Salāma 97; Ibn Ḥazm 62-63).

125 Q 76.8
they give food, for the love of Him, to the needy, the orphan, the captive:

Commentary: In this verse and its surrounding context, the righteous believers are held up as those who feed the needy, the orphans, and the captives because of their love of Allah and not for personal gain. Some commentators state that Q 76.8 is not abrogated; they consider this verse a spiritual principle that should be applied to the feeding of captives as well as the needy and orphans. Other commentators have argued, however, that Q 76.8 is abrogated (Ibn al-Jawzī, *Nawāsikh* 502).

NOTE: Most likely those commentators who support the abrogation of this verse base their position according to the doctrine of *al-walā' wa'l barā'* (loyalty and friendship vs. disavowal and enmity), one of the most important basic principles of Islam. In simple terms, this doctrine means that Muslims must love whom Allah loves and hate whom Allah hates. By imposing the hatred of non-Muslims, this principle, thus by extension, would prohibit any compassion toward non-Muslims, even those in captivity.

126 Q 76.24

***so be thou patient under the judgment of thy Lord**, and obey not one of them, sinner or unbeliever.*

Commentary: This verse commands Muḥammad to wait patiently for Allah's judgment on the wicked and not obey these sinners and unbelievers, but this mandate is abrogated by the Sword verse (Ibn Salāma 97; Ibn al-Jawzī, *Nawāsikh* 503).

127 Q 86.17

So give a respite to the disbelievers. Deal you gently with them for a while. (Hilâlî-Khân trans.)

Commentary: The verse commands Muḥammad to grant the disbelievers a delay, but this postponement for disbelievers is considered abrogated by the Sword verse (Ibn Salāma 99; Ibn al-Jawzī, *Nawāsikh* 506).

128 Q 88.22

thou art not charged to oversee them.

Commentary: The verse tells Muḥammad that he has no power over the disbelievers and is not their keeper, implying in later verses that Allah will determine the consequences of the wicked. According to some scholars, Muḥammad's limited role as just a messenger is abrogated by the Sword verse (Ibn Salāma 100; Ibn al-Jawzī, *Nawāsikh* 507; Ibn Ḥazm 65).

129 Q 109.6

To you your religion, and to me my religion!'

Commentary: Muḥammad's declaration in this verse means that he may freely practice his own religion and the non-Muslims (polytheists and People of the Book) may practice their own religion in peace; in other words, Muḥammad's words here suggest religious tolerance. However, this declaration is considered abrogated by the Sword verse (Ibn Salāma 104; Ibn al-Jawzī, *Nawāsikh* 509; Ibn Ḥazm 68).

Sword Verse Table Index

Topic	Issue	Abrogated Verse(s)
Allah		
	cursing of (by polytheists)	Q 6.108, Q 7.180
	final, only punisher	Q 6.158, Q 7.183, Q 10.46, Q 10.102, Q 13.40, Q 37.175, Q 74.11
	supreme, best judge	Q 10.109, Q 19.84, Q 22.68, Q 31.23, Q 34.25, Q 39.3, Q 39.46, Q 40.12, Q 52.48,
Christians—See **People of the Book**		
	avoidance of	Q 6.159
	forgiveness of	Q 2.109
	patience with	Q 3.186, Q 50.39
	peace with	Q 42.15
	tolerance of	Q 2.139, Q 42.15, Q 109.6
disbelievers—See **non-Muslims**		
family	enemy members	Q 64.14

Muḥammad		
	limited authority of	Q 4.80, Q 4.84, Q 6.66, Q 6.104, Q 6.107, Q 10.99, Q 10.108, Q 11.12, Q 17.54, Q 25.43, Q 39.41, Q 42.6, Q 42.48, Q 50.45, Q 88.22
	messenger only	Q 3.20, Q 5.99, Q 13.40, Q 16.82, Q 24.54, Q 42.48
	preaching of	Q 4.63, Q 16.125, Q 20.135, Q 34.25, Q 39.39
	response to critics, rejecters	Q 4.63, Q 6.68, Q 6.158, Q 10.41, Q 10.109, Q 11.122, Q 19.75, Q 19.84, Q 20.130, Q 22.68, Q 23.96, Q 25.63, Q 30.60, Q 31.23, Q 33.48, Q 36.76, Q 41.34, Q 43.83, Q 45.14, Q 46.35, Q 50.39, Q 51.54, Q 52.31, Q 52.45, Q 52.48, Q 53.29, Q 68.44, Q 70.5, Q 73.10, Q 74.11
	warner only	Q 11.12, Q 11.122, Q 15.89, Q 19.39, Q 22.49, Q 27.92, Q 29.50, Q 35.23, Q 38.70
nonbelievers—See **non-Muslims**		

non-Muslims		
	avoidance of	Q 6.68, Q 6.159, Q 32.30, Q 37.174, Q 37.178
	disregard of	Q 5.105, Q 6.112, Q 15.3, Q 15.88, Q 37.174, Q 37.178, Q 43.83, Q 53.29, Q 54.6, Q 74.11
	forgiveness of	Q 15.85
	jealousy of	Q 15.88
	patience with	Q 3.186, Q 10.109, Q 16.127, Q 23.96, Q 40.55, Q 40.77, Q 50.39, Q 52.48, Q 68.48, Q 70.5, Q 73.10, Q 76.24, Q 86.17
	peace with	Q 8.61, Q 23.96, Q 25.63, Q 28.55, Q 33.48, Q 41.34
	punishment of (by Allah)	Q 6.158, Q 10.46, Q 13.40, Q 39.3, Q 39.15, Q 43.83, Q 68.44
	religious tolerance of	Q 2.256, Q 6.104, Q 6.112, Q 6.135, Q 10.41, Q 10.108, Q 11.121, Q 23.54, Q 23.96, Q 28.55, Q 33.48, Q 39.15, Q 39.41, Q 109.6
	treatment of	Q 4.81, Q 16.106

People of the Book		
	avoidance of	Q 6.159
	forgiveness of	Q 2.109
	patience with	Q 3.186, Q 50.39
	tolerance of	Q 42.15, Q 109.6
polytheists		
	avoidance of	Q 3.28, Q 4.63, Q 6.68, Q 6.91, Q 6.106, Q 7.199, Q 32.30, Q 37.174, Q 37.178
	disregard of	Q 6.70, Q 7.180, Q 7.183, Q 15.3, Q 15.88, Q 15.94, Q 31.23, Q 37.174, Q 37.178, Q 39.39, Q 51.54, Q 52.45, Q 70.42
	forgiveness of	Q 15.85, Q 36.76, Q 43.89, Q 45.14
	jealousy of	Q 15.88
	patience with	Q 10.109, Q 16.127, Q 20.130, Q 23.96, Q 30.60, Q 40.55, Q 40.77, Q 46.35, Q 50.39, Q 86.17
	peace with	Q 8.61, Q 23.96, Q 33.48, Q 41.34, Q 43.89
	punishment of (by Allah)	Q 6.158, Q 10.46, Q 10.102, Q 13.40, Q 19.75, Q 37.175, Q 39.3, Q 39.15, Q 39.40, Q 52.45

unbelievers—See **non-Muslims**		
war—*See also* **fighting**		
	captives of	Q 47.4, Q 76.8
	cessation of	Q 2.192, Q 4.90
	duties, obligations of	Q 2.190, Q 2.191, Q 2.192, Q 2.217, Q 4.84, Q 16.126, Q 60.8, Q 60.9
	retaliation in	Q 16.126
women (Meccan)	marriage eligibility of	Q 60.10

Special Names and Terms

The following entries provide more information or clarification for asterisked names of Muslim people or Islamic concepts mentioned in this book.

‘Abdu, Muḥammad

AD 1849-1905

An Egyptian reformer and Muslim apologist, this significant Islamic scholar is considered a leading figure of Islamic Modernism, a movement that tried to reconcile Islam with modern Western values. Muḥammad ‘Imārah, who compiled and published Abdu’s entire collection of works, ranks ‘Abdu as one of three men who played a key role in the “renaissance, the rebirth and the revival that was initiated by the peoples of the East in the nineteenth century. They were the real giant starting point in that innovation that has distinguished...modern and contemporary life from the one that was prevailed in the East under the rule of the Mamālīk and the Ottoman Turks” (‘Imarah 1: 13).

Faḍlāllah, Muḥammad Ḥusayn

AD 1935-2010

Grand Ayatollah Muḥammad Ḥusayn Faḍlāllah was the top Shiite cleric in Lebanon at the time of his death, and his numerous writings and preachings inspired and influenced a generation of Islamic militants, including the founders of Hezbollah. Though he preferred gradual reforms to sudden revolution, he also supported the option of violent revolution and considered suicide bombing justifiable retaliation if Islam is attacked with advanced enemy weaponry. He rejected the separation of political and religious power as well as the restoration of the caliphate. Though he opposed American-brokered Arab-Israeli peace negotiations and desired the destruction of Israel, he condemned the September 11 attacks in the United States as acts of terrorism.

Quṭb, Sayīd

AD 1906-1966)

From a poor rural family, this Egyptian writer became one of the foremost figures in modern Sunni Islamic revivalism. Originally, Quṭb was an ardent secularist but eventually adopted many Islamist views. He joined the fundamentalist Muslim Brotherhood in Egypt, becoming a leading member in the 1950s and 1960s. Over time, Quṭb's writings have become the theoretical basis for many of today's radical Islamic groups, including al Qaeda.

abrogated verses

Abrogated verses are verses that have been annulled or overridden by another verse or verses. An abrogated verse can be classified into one of three kinds: verse whose wording remains in the Qur'ān but its ruling is abrogated by another verse; verse whose ruling remains in the *sharī'a* (Islamic law) but whose words are no longer in the Qur'ān; verse whose wording and ruling are no longer applicable—the words are no longer in the Qur'ān and its ruling is not in the *sharī'a*.

al-'Anṣār ("the Helpers")

Muḥammad and his followers, who were known as *al-Muhājirūn* ("the Emigrants"), migrated from Mecca to Medina in AH 1 (AD 622). The 'Anṣār were those tribesmen from the Aws and Khazraj among the people of Medina who supported Muḥammad. The 'Anṣār became Muslim and joined Muḥammad in his raids against the Quraysh.

Companion(s)

This term refers to those Muslims who accompanied Muḥammad for a long period of time.

Da'wa

This Arabic word means "call" and refers to the proselytization of Islam.

Emigrants (*al-Muhājirūn*)

This title applies to the early followers of Muḥammad, who emigrated with him from Mecca to Medina during the Hijra (AD 1/AD 622).

ḥadīth

The word *ḥadīth* can be translated as a speech, a saying, or even small talk. In Islamic theology, the term refers to a narrative concerning a deed or utterance of Muḥammad reported by his Companions.

Ḥadīth literature

These materials are the oral reports of Muḥammad's sayings and actions (circulated among his followers after his death) that were collected and written down. Two major collections of these *ḥadīths*, *Ṣaḥīḥ Bukhārī* and *Ṣaḥīḥ Muslim*, are considered by Sunni Muslims as the most authentic of these narrations. This literature, considered in importance second only to the Qur'ān, is routinely consulted concerning issues of Islamic law, ethics, and doctrine.

Hijra

Islam's prophet Muḥammad and his followers migrated from Mecca to Medina in June AD 622. The year that this journey took place was later designated the first year in the Islamic calendar, or AH 1.

hypocrite(s) (*al-munāfiqūn*)

The term "hypocrite" or "hypocrites" is mentioned several times in the Qur'ān. Indeed, one chapter of the Qur'ān (Q 63) is titled "The Hypocrites" (Al-Munāfiqūn). Anyone who displays faith (in this case, Islam) yet hides misbelief is considered a hypocrite (*al-munāfiq*). In Q 66.9 (see also Q 9.73, a fighting verse), Muḥammad is directed to "[s]trive hard against the disbelievers and the hypocrites, and be severe against them, their abode with be Hell,—and worst indeed is that destination" (Hilâlî-Khân trans.)

jizya (head tax)

It is the head tax imposed by Islamic law (*sharī'a*) on People of the Book (Christians and Jews) who do not embrace Islam as a religion. The purpose of the tax is to subdue and humiliate the payee. In return, payees can live and practice their own faith with some restrictions among Muslims in their community. (See Q 9.29: "Fight those who believe not in God and the Last Day and do not forbid what God and His Messenger have forbidden—such men as practise not the religion of truth, being of those who have been given the Book—until they pay the tribute out of hand and have been humbled.")

Meccan/Medinan periods

According to Islamic teachings, some portions of the Qur'ān were revealed to Muḥammad during his time in Mecca (Meccan period or Meccan Qur'ānic text) or in Medina (Medinan period or Medinan Qur'ānic text). These two main portions contrast markedly in terms of style, tone, and emphasis. The suras, or chapters, revealed during the earlier Meccan period are more personal, spiritual, and universal. All the pacifist verses were revealed during this earlier period. The later Medinan verses, which abrogate or nullify the Meccan verses, are less personal and more legalistic, prescribing rules on such matters as inheritance, familial and marital relationships, the property of orphans, gambling, food, and wine. These later revelations also include those verses that call believers to be harsh with unbelievers, to kill them wherever they find them.

occasion(s)

The Qur'ān, according to Islamic belief, is a book that "descended from heaven" in sections over a twenty-two-year period (AD 610-632). According to the exegetes, large parts of the Qur'ān descended in smaller portions as needed upon Muḥammad during his Da'wā. Furthermore, the Islamic commentators have established that many of the verses "descended" to address or respond to a particular issue or event and so the causes and details of these incidents that immediately preceded these revealed verses have been closely examined to determine their historical and social context. This special field of research is known as the science of *asbāb al-nuzūl* ("occasions or circumstances of revelation").

Endnotes

1. al-Zarkashī 354.
2. See Ibn Hishām 191. For the Arabic source, see Ibn Hishām 1: 416.
3. Ibid. 194. For the Arabic source, see Ibn Hishām 1: 424.
4. al-Ṭabarī 16: 574, 576.
5. Ibid. 17: 458.
6. al-Zamakhsharī 4: 352.
7. Ibn Hishām 286-288. For Arabic sources, see Ibn Hishām 1: 604 and al-Wāḥidī, *Asbāb* 71-72.
8. Ibid. 304. For the Arabic source, see Ibn Hishām 1: 635-636.
9. Ibid. For the Arabic source, see Ibn Hishām 1: 635-636.
10. See Ibn Hishām 664-665 and Ibn Sa'd 2: 111-112. For Arabic sources, see Ibn Hishām 2: 617 and Ibn Sa'd 2: 87.
11. al-Ya'qubī 1: 391; see also Ibn Hishām 665 and Ibn Sa'd 2: 112.
12. Ibn Hishām 665. For Arabic sources, see Ibn Hishām 2: 617 and Ibn Sa'd 2: 87, editor's footnote number 4.
13. Ibn Sa'd 2: 112. For the Arabic source, see Ibn Sa'd 2: 87.
14. Ibn Hishām 313-316. For the Arabic source, see Ibn Hishām 1: 654-656.
15. Ibid. 315. For the Arabic source, see Ibn Hishām 1: 654-655.
16. Ibid. For the Arabic source, see Ibn Hishām 1: 654.
17. Ibid. 316. For the Arabic source, see Ibn Hishām 1: 656.
18. Ibid. For the Arabic source, see Ibn Hishām 1: 657.
19. Ibid.
20. Ibn al-Naḥḥās 879.
21. al-Suyūṭī, *Asbāb* 74.
22. Ibn Kathīr, *al-Bidāyah* 7: 49; al-Wāḥidī, *Asbāb* 153.
23. al-Ṭabarī 6: 564; al-Suyūṭī, *Asbāb* 74.
24. al-Ṭabarī 6: 562.

25. al-Bahrani 2: 203.

26. al-Turmudhī 5: 3.

27. NOTE: For this verse Q 2.256, the Pickthall English translation is preferable to the Arberry translation, because it aligns more closely with the Arabic text and uses more contemporary English word choice and clearer syntax. (Arberry translation for Q 2.256: *No compulsion is there in religion. Rectitude has become clear from error. So whosoever disbelieves in idols and believes in God, has laid hold of the most firm handle, unbreaking; God is All-hearing, All-knowing.*) For additional comparison, see also the English translations of Yusuf Ali, Hilâlî-Khân, Sher Ali, Khalifa, Palmer, Rodwell, and Sale.

28. al-Suyūṭī, *Asbāb* 45-50.

29. al-Qurṭubī 4: 282.

30. Ibid. 4: 281.

31. al-Baghawī 1: 314; see also al-Ṭabarī 4: 548 and al-Suyūṭī, *al-Durr al-Manthūr* 3: 195.

32. al-Wāḥidī, *Asbāb* 86.

33. al-Ṭabarī 4: 553.

34. al-Wāḥidī, *Asbāb* 86.

35. Ibn Hishām 289. For the Arabic source, see Ibn Hishām 1: 550.

36. Ibid. 437. For the Arabic source, see Ibn Hishām 2: 190.

37. al-Baghawī 1: 314; see also al-Ṭabarī 4: 548 and al-Suyūṭī, *al-Durr al-Manthūr* 3: 195.

38. Ibn al-Jawzī, *Nawāsikh* 219 (Q 9.5); Ibn al-Jawzī, *Nawāsikh* 219; al-Makkī 193 (Q 9.73).

39. al-Baghawī 1: 314.

40. al-Ṭabarī 4: 551.

41. Ibid. 4: 552.

42. Ibn al-Jawzī, *Nawāsikh* 217; al-Makkī 193; al-Ṭabarī 4: 551.

43. Ibn al-Jawzī, *Nawāsikh* 220.

44. Ibid. 218, and *Zād al-Masīr* 1: 306.

45. al-Qurṭubī 4: 280-283; emphasis added.
46. al-Zarkashī 354.
47. al-Qurṭubī 10: 109-110.
48. Ibid. 10: 110.
49. 'Abdu 10: 198-199.
50. al-Ṭabarī 11: 343.
51. al-Ṭabāṭabā'ī 9: 156.
52. al-Ṭabarī 11: 343.
53. 'Abdu 10: 198-199.
54. Ṭabarsī 5: 13.
55. 'Abdu 10: 198-199.
56. al-Qurṭubī 1: 110-111.
57. al-Ṭabarī 11: 343.
58. al-Wāḥidī, *al-Tafsīr al-Basīṭ* 10: 294.
59. al-Ṭabarī 11: 343.
60. Ibid.
61. 'Abdu 10: 199.
62. Quṭb 1592.
63. Ibid. 1589.
64. Ibid. 1591.
65. Faḍlāllah 11: 25.
66. Ibid.
67. Ibn al-Jawzī, *Nawāsikh* 427.
68. Ibn 'Āshūr 10: 115.
69. al-Ṭabarī 16: 209.
70. al-Zamakhsharī 1: 310.
71. Ibn al-Jawzī, *Nawāsikh* 185; Ibn Kathīr, *Tafsīr* 2: 217.
72. Ibn al-Jawzī, *Nawāsikh* 179.
73. Ibid. 180.
74. Ibn Salāma 19; al-Makkī 155-156.

75. Ibn Kathīr, *Tafsīr* 7: 178; see also al-Ṭabarī 11: 421.

76. al-Ṭabarī 7: 121. For the occasion of this passage, see al-Baghawī 2: 231.

77. al-Bayḍāwī 4: 449.

78. al-Zamakhsharī 3: 30-31; compare with Ibn Kathīr, *al-Bidāyah* 7: 174.

79. *Sahih Bukhari*: vol. 4, bk. 52, no. 288.

80. Mālik Ibn Anas 5: 1314 (Book al-Jami', Section Name Ma Ja' fi al-Yahud [what was mentioned about Jews].

81. Khālid 29.

82. al-Marāghī 10: 58.

83. Quṭb 1546-1547.

84. "Iraqi Christians Flee after ISIS Issue Mosul Ultimatum;" see also Evans and al-Rube'i "Convert, Pay Tax, or Die, Islamic State Warns Christians" and "Christians Flee Mosul after ISIS Ultimatum to Convert or Leave." For additional discussion on the tax (*jizya*), see Erb "Islamic State Warns Christians: Convert, Pay Tax, Leave or Die." Islamic State (IS) later intensified their ultimatum by committing "acts of inhumanity on an unimaginable scale" (beheadings, killings, forced conversions, slavery and sexual abuse), according to the United Nations; see "UN to Send Investigators to Iraq over Islamic State 'Atrocities.'"

Bibliography

'Abdu, Muḥammad. *Tafsīr al-Qur'an al-Karim* [*Tafsīr al-Manār*]. Comp. Muḥammad Rashīd Riḍā.12 vols. Cairo: n.p., AH 1366/AD 1947. Print.

Ali, 'Abdullah Yusuf, trans. *The Holy Qur'an: Text Translation and Commentary.* 3rd ed. Lahore: Sh. Muḥammad Ashraf, AH 1356/ AD 1938, Print.

Arberry, Arthur J., trans. *The Koran Interpreted.* New York: MacMillan, AD 1955. Print.
NOTE: Unless an alternate source is provided, all English translations of verses cited in this book are based on the Arberry translation and will be indicated with italicized text.

al-Baghawī, Abū Muḥammad al-Ḥusayn Ibn Mas'ūd. *Tafsīr al-Baghawī* [a.k.a. *Ma'ālim al-Tanzīl*]. 8 vols. Riyadh: Dār Tība, AH 1409/ AD 1989. Print.

al-Baḥrānī, Hāshim. *al-Burhan fi Tafsīr al-Qur'ān.* 8 vols. Beirut: al-A'lamī, AH 1427/AD 2006. Print.

al-Bayḍāwī, Abū Sa'īd 'Abdullah Ibn 'Umar. *Tafsīr al-Qādī al-Bayḍāwī.* Ed. Muḥammad 'Abd al-Qādir Shāhīn. 8 vols. Beirut: Dār al-Kutub al-'Ilmīya, AH 1419/AD 1999. Print.

"Christians Flee Mosul after ISIS Ultimatum to Convert or Leave." *Al Arabiya News.* Al Arabiya News, 18 July 2014. Web. 21 July 2014. <http://english.alarabiya.net/en/News/middle-east/2014/07/18/Christians-flee-Mosul-after-ISIS-ultimatum-to-convert-or-leave.html>.

Erb, Kelly Phillips. "Islamic State Warns Christians: Convert, Pay Tax, Leave Or Die." *Forbes.com.* Forbes, 19 July 2014. Web. 10 Dec. 2014. <http://www.forbes.com/sites/kellyphillipserb/2014/07/19/islamic-state-warns-christians-convert-pay-tax-leave-or-die/>.

Evans, Dominic and Isra' al-Rube'i. "Convert, Pay Tax, or Die, Islamic State Warns Christians." *Reuters.com.* Reuters, 18 July 2014. Web. 10 Dec. 2014. <http://www.reuters.com/article/2014/07/18/us-iraq-security-christians-idUSKBN0FN29J20140718>.

Faḍlāllah, Muḥammad Ḥusayn. *Tafsīr min Waḥī al-Qur'ān.* 24 vols. Beirut: Dār al-Malāk, AD 1998. Print.

al-Hilâlî, Muḥammad Taqî-ud-Dîn and Muḥammad Muḥsin Khân, trans. 4th ed. *The Noble Qur'ān.* Riyadh: Dar-us-Salam, AD 1993. Print.

Ibn 'Āshūr, Muḥammad al-Ṭahīr. *Tafsīr al-Taḥrīr wa al-Tanwīr.* 30 vols. Tunis: al-Dār al-Tunisīya, AD 1984. Print.

Ibn Ḥazm, Abū 'Abd Allah Muḥammad. *al-Nāsikh wa al-Mansūkh fī al-Qur'ān al-Karīm.* Ed. 'Abdul-Ghaffār Sulayimān al-Bendārī. Beirut: Dār al-Kutub al-'Ilmīya, AH 1406/AD 1986. Print.

Ibn Hishām, 'Abd al-Malik al-Ma'āfrī. *al-Sīra al-Nabawīya l-Ibn Hishām.* Eds. Muṣṭafā al-Saqqā, Ibrāhīm al-Ibīāry, and 'Abd al-Ḥafīz Shalabī. 2 vols. Damascus: Dār Ibn Kathīr, n.d. Print. (Arabic)

Ibn Hishām, 'Abd al-Malik, Ed. *The Life of Muḥammad: A Translation of Ishāq's* Sīrat Rasūl Allāh. Trans., introd. and notes by A. Guillaume. Karachi: Oxford UP, AH 1386/AD 1967. Print. (English)

Ibn al-Jawzī, Abū al-Faraj 'Abd al-Raḥman. *Nawāsikh al-Qur'ān.* Ed. Muḥammad Ashraf 'Alī al-Milbārī. Medina: al-Majlis al-'Ilmī, AH 1404/AD 1984. Print.

—. *Zād al-Masīr fī 'Ilm al-Tafsīr.* 4 vols. Beirut: al-Maktab al-Islāmī, AH 1404/AD 1984. Print.

Ibn Kathīr, Ismāil. *al-Bidāyah wa al-Nihāyah* [a.k.a. *Tārīkh Ibn Kathīr*]. Ed. 'Abd Allah Ibn 'Abd al-Muḥsin al-Turkī. 21 vols. Giza: Hagr printing, AH 1417-1419/AD 1997-1999. Print.

—. *Tafsīr al-Qur'ān al-'Azīm.* Ed. Muṣṭafā al-Sayīd Muḥammad, et al. 15 vols. Giza: Qurṭuba Est., AH 1420/AD 2000. Print.

Ibn Manzūr. *Lisān al-'Arab.* Eds. 'Abd Allah 'Alī al-Kabīr, Muḥammad Aḥmad Ḥassab Allah, and Hāshīm Muḥammad al-Shādhlī. Cairo: Dār al-Ma'ārif, n.d. Print.

Ibn al-Naḥḥās, Aḥmad Ibn Ibrāhīm Ibn Muḥammad. *Mashāri' al-Ashwāq ilā Maṣāri' al-'Ushāq: Wa Muthīr al-Gharām ilā Dār al-Salām.* Ed. Idrīs Muḥammad 'Alī and Muḥammad Khālīd Istānbullī. 3rd ed. Beirut: Dār al-Bashā'r al-Islāmīya, AH 1423/AD 2002. Print.

Ibn Sa'd, [Muḥammad]. *Kitab al-Tabaqat al-Kabir.* Trans. S. Moinul Haq. 2 vols. New Delhi: Kitab Bhavan, AH 1410/AD 1990. Print. (English)

Ibn Sa'd, Muḥammad. *Kitāb al-Ṭabaqāt al-Kabīr.* Ed. 'Alī Muḥammad 'Umar. 11 vols. Cairo: al-Khānjī, AH 1421/AD 2001. Print. (Arabic)

Ibn Salāma, Abū al-Qāsim Hibat Allah. *al-Nāsikh wa al-Mansūkh.* Ed. Māhir 'Abd al-'Azīm al-Ṭantāwī. Beirut: Dār al-Yusef, n.d. Print.

'Imārah, Muḥammad, ed. *The Entire Works of Imām Sheīkh Muḥammad 'Abdu.* 5 vols. Cairo: Dār al-Shurūq, AD 1993. Print.

"Iraqi Christians Flee after ISIS Issue Mosul Ultimatum." *BBC.* BBC News, 18 July 2014. Web. 21 July 2014. <http://www.bbc.com/news/world-middle-east-28381455>.

Khālid, Hassan. *The Position of the Prophet on the Three Religions: Idolatry, Judaism and Christianity.* Cairo: Dār al-Kitāb al-Islāmī, n.d. Print.

al-Makkī, Abū Muḥammad Ibn Abī Ṭālib. *al-Iḍāh li-Nāsikh al-Qur'ān wa Mansūkhuhu wa Ma'rifat Usūluhu wa Ikhtilāf al-Nāss Fīhi.* Ed. Aḥmad Hassan Faraḥāt. Jeddah: Dār al-Manāra, AH 1406/AD 1986. Print.

Mālik Ibn Anas. *Muwaṭṭā' al-Imām Mālik.* Ed. Muḥammad Muṣṭafā al-A'ẓamī. 8 vols. Abū Dhabī: Zayed Foundation, AD 2004. Print.

al-Marāghī, Muḥammad Muṣṭafā. *Tafsīr al-Marāghī.* Cairo: Muṣṭafā al-Bābī al-Ḥalabī, AD 1946. Print.

al-Naḥḥās, Abū Ja'far Muḥammad Ibn Aḥmad. *al-Nāsikh wa al-Mansūkh fī Kitāb Allah 'Azza wa Jalla wa Ikhtilāf al-'Ulamā' fī Dhalik.* Ed. Sulaymān Ibrāhīm Ibn 'Abd Allah al-Lāḥim. 3 vols. Cairo: al-Risāla, AH 1412/AD 1991. Print.

Pickthall, Marmaduke, trans. *The Meaning of the Glorious Quran.* AD 1930. *Global Grey.* Web. 13 Mar. 2015. <http://www.globalgrey.co.uk>.

al-Qurṭubī, Abū 'Abd Allah Muḥammad Ibn Aḥmad. *al-Jāmi' li-Aḥkām al-Qur'ān wa al-Mubayīn li-mā Taḍammanahu min al-Sunna wa Āay al-Furqān.* Ed. 'Abd Allah Ibn 'Abd al-Muḥsin al-Turkī. 24 vols. Beirut: al-Risāla, AH 1427/AD 2006. Print.

Quṭb, Sayīd. *Fī Ẓilāl al-Qur'ān.* 32nd official ed. Cairo: Dār al-Shurūq, AH 1423/AD 2003. Print.

Sahih Bukhari. Trans. M. Muḥsin Khan. Ed. Mika'il al-Amany. 1st ed. 9 vols. 2 Oct. 2009. *IslamHouse.com*. N.p. Web. Apr. 2012. <http://d1.islamhouse.com/data/en/ih_books/single/en_Sahih_Al-Bukhari.pdf>.

Sale, George, trans. *The Koran: Commonly Called the Alcoran of Mohammad*. 5th ed. Philadelphia: J. W. Moore, 1856. *Google books*. Web. July 2014. <http://books.google.com/books?id=6osxHeW6XDsC&output=pdf>.

Sale, George, trans. *The Koran: Commonly Called the Alkoran of Mohammad*. London: F. Warne, n.d. Print.

Shu'la, Abū 'Abd Allah. *Ṣafwat al-Rāsikh fī 'Ilm al-Mansūkh wa al-Nāsikh*. Ed. Muḥammad Ibrāhīm 'Abd al-Raḥman Fāris. Cairo: al-Thaqāfa al-Dīnīya, AH 1415/AD 1995. Print.

al-Suyūṭī, Jalāl al-Dīn 'Abd al-Raḥman. *Asbāb al-Nuzūl* [a.k.a. *Lubāb al-Nuqūl fī Asbāb al-Nuzūl*]. Beirut: Dār al-Kitāb al-'Arabī, AH 1426/AD 2006. Print.

—. *al-Durr al-Manthūr fī al-Tafsīr bi-l-Ma'thūr*. Ed. 'Abd Allah Ibn 'Abd al-Muḥsin al-Turkī. 17 vols. Cairo: Hajr Center, AH 1424/AD 2003. Print.

al-Ṭabarī, Abū Ja'far Muḥammad Ibn Jarīr. *Jāmi' al-Bayān 'an Ta'wīl Āay al-Qur'ān* [a.k.a. *Tafsīr al-Ṭabarī*]. Ed. 'Abd Allah Ibn 'Abd al-Muḥsin al-Turkī. 26 vols. Cairo: Hajr Center, AH 1422/AD 2001. Print.

Ṭabarsī, al-Fadl Ibn al-Ḥasan. *Majma' al-Bayān fī Tafsīr al-Qur'ān*. 10 vols. Beirut: Dār al-'Ulum, Dār al-Murtaḍā, AD 2006. Print.

al-Ṭabāṭabā'ī, Muḥammad Ḥusayn. *al-Mīzān fī Tafsīr al-Qur'ān*. Ed. Ḥusayn al-A'lā. 21 vols. Beirut: al-A'lamī, AD 1997. Print.

al-Turmudhī, Abū 'Isā Muḥammad Ibn 'Isā. *al-Jāmi' al-Ṣaḥīḥ* [a.k.a. *Sunan al-Turmudhī*]. Ed. Aḥmad Muḥammad Shākir. 2nd ed. Egypt: Muṣṭafā al-Bābī al-Ḥalabī. AH 1398/AD 1978. Print.

"UN to Send Investigators to Iraq over Islamic State 'Atrocities.'" *The Guardian*. 1 Sept. 2014. Web. 11 Sept. 2014. <http://www.theguardian.com/world/2014/sep/01/un-investigators-iraq-islamic-state-atrocities>.

al-Wāḥidī, Abū al-Ḥasan 'Alī Ibn Aḥmad. *Asbāb Nuzūl al-Qur'ān*. Ed. Kamāl Basyūnī Zaghlūl. Beirut: Dār al-Kutub al-'Ilmīya, AH 1411/ AD 1991. Print.

—. *al-Tafsīr al-Basīṭ*. Ed. Ibrāhīm Ibn 'Alī al-Ḥasan. 25 vols. Riyadh: Imām Muḥammad Ibn S'ūd Islamic UP, AH 1430/AD 2014. Print.

al-Ya'qubī [Aḥmad Ibn Abū Ya'qub Ibn Waḍiḥ]. *Tarīkh al-Ya'qubī*. Ed. 'Abd al-Amīr Mahanna. 2 vols. Beirut: al-A'lamī, AH 1431/ AD 2010. Print.

al-Zamakhsharī, Jār Allah Abū al-Qāsim Maḥmūd Ibn 'Umar. *al-Kashāf 'an Haqā'iq Ghumūḍ al-Tanzīl wa 'Uyūn al-Aqāwil fī Wujūh al-Ta'wīl*. Ed. 'Ādil Aḥmad 'Abd al-Mawjūd and 'Alī Muḥammad Mu'awaḍ. 5 vols. Riyadh: al-'Ubaykān, AH 1418/AD 1998. Print.

al-Zarkashī, Abū 'Abd Allah Badr al-Dīn. *al-Burhān fī 'Ulūm al-Qur'ān*. 3rd ed. Ed. Muḥammad Abū al-Faḍl Ibrāhīm. 4 vols. Cairo: Dār al-Turāth, AH 1404/AD 1984. Print.

Name Index

Note that only contemporary names have been alphabetized by last name.

‡ These marked entries in the Name and Subject Indexes are also included in the Sword Verse Table Index, pages 99-105. These topics and their specific issues listed there are referenced to applicable abrogated verses in the Qur'ān.

Subject Index

‡ These marked entries in the Name and Subject Indexes are also included in the Sword Verse Table Index, pages 99-105. These topics and their specific issues listed there are referenced to applicable abrogated verses in the Qur'ān.